KT-366-347

GORDON RUPP

The Sixty Plus
and other Sermons

COLLINS
Fount Paperbacks

First published in Fount Paperbacks, 1978

© Gordon Rupp 1978

Made and printed in Great Britain by
William Collins Sons & Co. Ltd, Glasgow

The Sixty Plus and other Sermons

Gordon Rupp is Emeritus Professor of Ecclesiastical History in the University of Cambridge, a Doctor of Divinity of Cambridge, Aberdeen and Paris, and a Fellow of the British Academy. He entered the Methodist ministry in 1938 and was minister during the war years in Chislehurst, Kent. He then taught Church History in Richmond College, London and in the University of Manchester, returning to Cambridge in 1967. In 1968 he was President of the Methodist Conference, and for some years a member of the Central Committee of the World Council of Churches.

By the same author

THOMAS MORE (Collins)

Contents

Preface

Life has its own ways of setting examinations for us, and every ten years or so most of us find ourselves in new situations, which in turn ask new questions of our faith. Around our 'Sixty Plus' we meet a whole group of them – growing older, meeting pain and illness, separation and bereavement, death. These experiences come to all of us, to people of all religions and of none, and we all have to learn to live with them, with courage, cheerfulness and dignity, and if we are Christians, with hope. What is the meaning of that hope? In our time very much is being done for the material and even the psychological welfare of the elderly, but perhaps not so much for their religious and theological needs. The first four sermons in this little book tried to tackle those needs in a rather simple way, and the unexpectedly warm response seemed to show that there are many who would welcome such counsel in these days. I have added some readings which are entitled 'Comfortable Words', from those who are entitled to speak to us from personal experiences they have undergone, and I have intended the word 'comfortable' to be understood in its original meaning of encouraging and strengthening rather than as sedative and soothing.

The other sermons have been preached on different occasions in the last few years, in large churches and in small chapels, by one whose one consistent vocation has been that of a Methodist preacher, and what virtue is in them comes from that vast sea of faces whom I gratefully and affectionately remember, and of course, the divine cheerfulness which has again and again come breaking in, notably in the great hymns of Isaac Watts and Charles Wesley.

Ash Wednesday, 1978

Part One

I

Growing Younger

2 Corinthians 4:16. *Wherefore we are not wearied, but though our outward man perish, yet the inward man is renewed day by day.*

William Tyndale, 1526

Over the pavilion at Lord's Cricket Ground there is the famous weather-vane showing Father Time bending down, taking off the bails from the stumps, at close of play. And for those of us, after the tea interval of life, as we watch the lengthening shadows over the grass, it beckons for our attention. For there comes a time when we realize that we are running out of steam and out of time. We find our friends asking about our retirement, and before we know it, there it is, on our own doorstep. We forget people's names more easily – old age? Little brown spots appear on our hands – old age! Well, we should have known it must happen, though we hardly realized it when we heard the schoolboy song:

> Forty years on, growing older and older
> Shorter in wind, as in memory long

> What will it help you that once you
> were strong?

Of course, our bodies have always been wearing out, all our lives, and it has been said that our mental powers

11

diminish from about the age of sixteen. But now the only replacements seem to be artificial ones, and the 'sans teeth', 'sans eyes' of the last act of man on the human stage suggests that even the artificial aids offered by the Welfare State may outlive their use. We get puffed more easily, we prefer Scrabble to mountaineering, and we understand why Francis spoke of 'Brother Ass'. 'A lot of my contemporaries who used to look like grapes now look like raisins,' somebody said. If a boy knows about growing pains, then, at the other end of life, there are what we might call 'shrinking pains'.

With all these things come new situations. For some retirement is a big issue, for it means at least the drastic reordering of our use of time – and money. It may mean pulling up roots and finding new places to live – always a minor crisis at any time in life. It means probably less income at a time when we could do with rather more, not fewer, creature comforts. Old spiritual foes, whom we thought we had got the better of long ago, now raise their ugly heads – a new form of 'identity crisis' is upon us.

I read recently the results of a psychological quiz conducted in California with scores of people aged eighty-five and over. (The investigators both died young, before their results could be published, which I suppose proves something!)

They distinguished three groups of people: the Angry Ones, the Rocking Chair People and the Mature. The Angry Ones were pathetic and disturbing, because we have all met people who seem to have become sour and embittered, disillusioned and resentful, as they grow old. They have accumulated frustrations, they are nostalgic or guilty, they become a trial to those about them, and their tempers range from general grumpiness to downright nastiness. And if we are honest, we shall admit there is something of this in all of us. It is sad when anybody gets like this, for such unhappiness is contagious.

The Rocking Chair People are the ones who have just caved in, and given up. They did their whack with life and now it is up to the others. They want to relax and no great cause, no struggles, enlist their interest any more. Seaside resorts are full of retired people who want no more jobs, who even conceal the fact that they spent the best years of their life in leadership in church and community. All very understandable, but it would be wrong to let this attitude spill over into our thoughts of how Christians are to behave when growing older.

There are, of course, some mental gimmicks: as the old phrase says, 'Accept yourself. Be yourself.' Accept the life you have had, for it cannot be altered, and you cannot have it again. Indeed, as J. M. Barrie's *Mary Rose* suggested, it would probably not come out very differently if you could. You simply have to accept it, realizing that at this moment your evaluation of what you have been and what you have done is likely to be very one-sided, and, from the Christian point of view, almost irrelevant. Accept too, the fact that nobody is indispensable, that our job, our church, our world, will go on without us and that others can and must take over, and that this has been true for all men and women from the beginning. Then you can apply those Christian and healing salves: forgiveness and gratitude. We can take God's forgiveness for so much wasted and done amiss, and because God has forgiven us we can forgive ourselves (and this is for some people the harder thing). And we can cultivate the art of gratitude. The General Thanksgiving is one prayer we dare not omit.

There were two great German theologians early in this century, one of whom seemed always in the dumps. So the great Adolf von Harnack wrote to the great Karl Holl:

I wish you would unlearn your fatal trick of turning every fruit tree that God sends you into a weeping willow.

What is the use of all our Christianity if it doesn't give us a cheerful countenance and the power to meet suffering with manly courage? And are the tribulations which get you down really so great? Shall I add up your possessions – good things, trusted friends, ability to work – so that you are in duty bound to joy and thankfulness? And to spread joy and humour around you. You ought not to be miserable even if cannons were roaring all round you and you had to go out under fire. This is your moral duty. It is even more important than the Ten Commandments!

My own first wall against despondency is to say, 'Lord, I am not worthy of the least of all thy mercies'. My second is not to take life too seriously, but with a pinch of humour. My third, to remind myself that there are human beings to whom I matter – even if it is just one human being, one little child. With those three walls you can shelter against a whole sea of storms, and keep that joyful courage which is the one essential ground of our existence.

Sound advice, from one old man of thirty-five to

another old fellow of thirty-two!

But when we begin to think as Christians, the upside-down language of the Kingdom of God takes over. Here, in Christ, we do not grow older, but we actually grow younger. 'Though our outward man perishes, yet the inward man is renewed day by day.' There is a poignant moment in Shakespeare when Mark Antony has lost the great battle and feels his age, and for the last time he takes off his shining armour. 'Unarm Eros: the long day's task is done.' No, says St Paul, 'Now is our salvation nearer than when we believed. The night is far spent, the day is at hand: let us therefore cast off the works of darkness, and let us put on the armour of light.'

There's a story of two old Chelsea Pensioners who were talking. One of them said, 'Do you remember the stuff they used to put in our food when we were cadets, to stop us thinking too much about girls?' 'Yes.' 'Well, in my case I think it's just beginning to work.' This is the moment in our Christian existence to say to ourselves: 'Remember all those things which were muttered over our heads when we were christened? Well, I really believe they are beginning to come true!'

Go back to the service of Holy Baptism which was said for you as a child. It is all upside-down talk, all back-to-front experience. You began as a Christian, not with baby-talk, but with the thought of death and dying – you were baptized into the death of Christ, and you rose again to new life. You began old – that quaint stuff about the 'old Adam' beginning to die in you. Indeed Christianity is not a better life but a new life. This is no flummery of mystical words, no flowery metaphor. When Christ died and rose again, something happened not only for himself, but for all of those who believe in him. His love catches us up in a new kind of existence – that X-Dimension where we live together with him and with all others who enter into this experience – a life which lies beyond, and under the surface of our daily life and yet which interpenetrates the workaday present life in the world. By faith we enter into this existence, and in each successive moment we encounter God, in a relationship which is as creative as it is spontaneous, and which brings with it joy and creative energy. Luther says faith is like boiling water – which is still the same, and yet all of which is changed when it boils. From that moment of baptism we begin to grow our resurrection body, for it is with us as with tadpoles and caterpillars, that our growing personalities will need new instruments for the kinds of existence God has in store for us.

Life really is what Keats called it. 'a vale of soul making'. We are here to grow as persons, out of the Old Adam, the unmade, twisted, environment plus heredity with which we begin, into the new man in Christ. This point, then, our retirement, should be the moment to recollect what our lives have Christianly always been about, and that the end product is for us to enter into the Kingdom of Heaven as little children. But we are beloved children, not discarded, worn-out tools. The underlying, fundamental truth about us has not been the importance of our job, our daily work, our spare-time hobbies or service of good and great causes, but that what God has done for us and in us is the all-important thing. We have never been to him an instrument only, a twig in a broom with which to sweep a dirty world, but we are children.

Another thing about that baptism service. It was realistic. There was a whiff of gunpowder about it. It was not a romantic, fairy-tale gloss on real life, or if it was, there were wicked fairies present. There were those odd words to use about a baby, about being Christ's faithful soldier, unto our life's end. The seventeenth century had a wonderful word, 'footmanship'. The footman was the long-distance runner. Bunyan in his lovely tract, *The Heavenly Footman*, warns Christians:

> The way is long, and there is many a dirty step, many a high hill, much work to do, a wicked heart, world and devil to overcome. Thou must run a long and tedious journey . . . before you come to the land of promise . . . Perseverance is a great part of the Cross.

There are some lovely green gardens at the foot of the dusty rock of Gibraltar. Here it was that they brought the wounded crew of the *Victory* after the Battle of Trafalgar. After the fight a great storm arose, and the battered ship, dismasted, and with torn sails, crawled into harbour. That is how a great Christian hymn-writer described the last bit of the Christian life.

> Safe home, safe home in port!
> Rent cordage, shattered deck,
> Torn sails, provisions short,
> And only not a wreck;
> But O the joy upon the shore
> To tell the voyage-perils o'er!

That ninth-century writer, Joseph the Hymnographer, takes up St Paul's metaphor, the athlete competing in the games:

The prize, the prize secure!
The athlete nearly fell;
Bare all he could endure,
And bare not always well:
But he may smile at troubles gone
Who sets the victor-garland on.

So God treats our lives with infinite respect and gives them dignity at the very point when they might seem rather comic and pathetic. This indeed may be one of the hardest fights of our lives, the really deadly moment of temptation for which Luther had a special word, '*Anfechtung*', because its undertone suggested a fight – the moment when we might relax too soon, give up the good fight of faith, succumb to new experiences which now crowd together: pain, separation, loneliness, weakness, failing powers. But faith, God assures us, has great things in store: there are surprises, new discoveries, new victories:

There is good news yet to hear
And fine things to be seen
Before we go to Paradise
By way of Kensal Green.
(G. K. Chesterton)

This last lap is a necessary, indispensable stage in the finishing of one of God's masterpieces, a human being.

Seen in this way, time becomes even more precious, for we begin to understand what St Paul means by 'buying up' or 'redeeming the time', and what Kipling meant by filling the unforgiving minute with sixty seconds' worth of distance run. We can no longer treat the months and days with carelessness as though we had an unlimited store of them. And in a sense we redeem past time, for it becomes something not to resent, or to forget, because those experiences and the people who gave us past joy are gone, for these very things become something to hope about.

I found the book *Poet's Progress*, which is about Siegfried Sassoon, helpful at this point. It is about his experiences after he became a Christian in 1965 at the age of seventy-one. He has movingly told the story of his earlier life in a series of essays. As a young officer in World War I he shared with the generation of Rupert Brooke and Wilfred Owen a high idealism which gradually withered in the face of the senseless waste and cruelty of modern war. He was a brave soldier, but there came a moment when, in bitterness, he flung his M.C. into the river Mersey. After 1965 he lived for ten years as a Christian and his journal, poems and letters during that time show how the grace of God not only made sense of the new experiences, but took up all his previous life and gave it new meaning:

> For grace in me divined
> This metaphor I find:
> A tree.
>   How can that be?
>
> This tree all winter through
> Found no green work to do –
> No life
>   Therein ran rife.
>
> But with an awoken year
> What surge of sap is here –
> What flood
>   In branch and bud.

So grace in me can hide –
Be darkened and denied –
Then once again
Vesture my every vein.

During those war years he had never been able to
pray. Now he saw that though he had not thought he
was walking with God, God all the time had been walking with him. And now in his old age, with a failing
body, with falls and tumbles, and where having his
teeth out was a major event, he was making each day
new discoveries, experiencing new moments of truth,
he made new poetry. He had discovered that wonderful
generosity of which Jesus spoke, where those who went
into the vineyard at the very last moment, at the
eleventh hour, got the full reward, and where, with
the loneliness of a long-distance runner, the prodigal
son stumbles at last over the threshold into a waiting
home, and hears the words, 'Bring forth the best robe
and put it on him!'

One of the noblest Germans of this century was
Count Helmuth James von Moltke. He was the descen-
dant of a great military family but he himself had
grown to hate all violence, and though he was committed
to the resistance to Hitler, he would take no part in
any plot to assassinate him. But he too was arrested in
the aftermath of that plot, and was executed in January
1945. His last letters to his wife and children are a
little anthology of Christian hope, and they too echo
what was the experience of Siegfried Sassoon, that when,
at the very last, God shows himself to us, it makes sense
of all our past pilgrimage:

I just wept a little, not because I was sad or melancholy, not because I wanted to turn back, but from

an intensity of gratitude at this proof of God's presence. It is not given to us to see him face to face, but we must needs be overwhelmed when we suddenly realize that he has gone before us all our lives through, as a pillar of cloud by day and of fire by night, and that in a flash, he suddenly lets us see it. Now there is nothing more to happen.

So we look eagerly and expectantly at the things which are unseen and eternal, for we believe that our light affliction, which is but for a moment, works for us an eternal weight of glory.

COMFORTABLE WORDS

CHRISTIAN. Is this the way to the Celestial City?
SHEPHERD. You are just in your way.
CHRISTIAN. How far is it thither?
SHEPHERD. Too far for any, but those that shall get thither indeed.

> John Bunyan, *The Pilgrim's Progress*

The way is long, and there is many a dirty step, many a high hill, much work to do, a wicked heart, world and devil to be overcome: I say, there are many steps to be taken by those that intend to be saved, by running or walking.

They that will go to heaven, they must run for it: because as the way is long, so the time in which they are to get to the end of it is very uncertain. The time present is the only time: thou hast not more time allotted to thee than that thou now enjoyest. Do not say I have time enough to get to heaven seven years hence: for I tell thee, the bell may toll for thee before seven days are ended: and therefore look to it, make no delays, it is not good dallying with things of so great concernment as the salvation of thy soul.

John Bunyan, *The Heavenly Footman*

To have entered and now to have completed my eightieth year does not cause me any anxiety: in fact, it helps to keep me serene and confident. As always I desire nothing more or less than what the Lord continues to give me. I thank and bless Him every day and I am ready for anything. I notice in my body the beginning of some trouble that must be natural for an old man. I bear it with resignation, even if it is sometimes rather tiresome and also makes me afraid it will get worse. It is not pleasant to think about this: but once more, I am prepared for anything. It gives me joy to be faithful to my religious practices, my constant preoccupation with God and with spiritual things. But above all I must endeavour to seek closer union with the Lord, and to keep myself in serene and loving converse with him.

Pope John XXIII, *Journal of a Soul*

Lord, thou knowest better than I know myself that I am growing older, and will some day be old. Keep me from the fatal habit of thinking that I must say something on every subject and on every occasion. Release me from the craving to straighten out everybody's affairs. Make me thoughtful but not moody: helpful but not bossy. With my vast store of wisdom it seems a pity not to use it all, but thou knowest, Lord, that I want a few friends at the end. Keep my mind free from the recital of endless details: give me wings to get to the point. Seal my lips on my aches and pains. They **are** increasing, and love of rehearsing them is becoming sweeter as the years go by. I dare not ask for grace enough to enjoy the tales of others' pains, but help me to endure them with patience.

I dare not ask for improved memory, but for a growing humility and a lessening cocksureness when my memory seems to clash with the memories of others. Teach me the glorious lesson that occasionally I may be mistaken.

Keep me reasonably sweet: I do not want to be a saint – some of them are so hard to live with, but a sour old person is one of the crowning works of the devil. Give me the ability to see good things in unexpected places and talents in unexpected people. And give me, O Lord, the grace to tell them so.

Anon. 'A Nun's Prayer'

These things I see, not with outward eyes and I do not hear them with outward hearing. I see them much more in my soul alone, while my eyes are open . . . the Light which I see is not tied to the things of space. It is much, much brighter than a cloud in which the sun is shining. It has not height or length or breadth. It seems to me to be the shadow of the living light. And in this light, sometimes, I see a greater light, which I call the Living Light. When and how I see this, I cannot tell. But as long as I see this light, all sadness and anxiety flee away and I feel myself to be once more a young girl of seventeen and not an old woman any more.

Saint Hildegarde of Bingen (1098–1179)

Pain and Counterpane

*2 Corinthians 1:3-5. Blessed be the God and Father of
Our Lord Jesus Christ, the Father of tender mercies and
the God of all comfort, who comforts me in all my distress,
so that I am able to comfort people who are in any
distress, by the comfort wherewith I myself am comforted
by God. For as the sufferings of Christ are abundant in
my case, so my comfort is also abundant through Christ.*
Dr Moffat's Translation

We are a talkative lot on the little bus which takes us
into town each morning. The passengers are mostly
ladies, 'bedders' in the colleges and shop assistants,
and the busy chatter sometimes sounds like a lot of
budgerigars. But later in the morning, coming back
from part-time jobs, the older ones talk about serious
things and sometimes I have been almost frozen in my
seat as I have overheard them talk about what has
just happened to them and their families: broken
hearts, homes, bodies – 'my daughter', 'my husband',
'my son'. It all comes out in a normal everyday voice
which makes it even more poignant. For they are a
very decent lot of people and they cope with life with a
courage and humour of which they are completely
unaware. They seem to have little connection with the
Church, and are perhaps a warning to Christians who
sometimes glibly assume they have all the answers;
for here are people who have at least got all the questions, probed more deeply in anxiety and pain, coping
with human resources, unfortified by the consolations

of religion. They find their resources of human courage and humour in a secular way. 'Our saints,' said Sheila Hancock, telling how she and her husband faced his last illness, 'were Morecambe and Wise.' Nor may we drive a wedge between human life and religion, since all courage, all true humour, come from God who is at hand for all his children in their every experience of life and death.

Just near our bus stop is a lovely Norman building, which in the twelfth century was the chapel of a leper hospital. There, savagely isolated by a frightened world, lived the victims of a terrible group of incurable diseases for whom medically the age could do almost nothing, save offer spiritual comfort – which perhaps is why the chapel has survived. Rather strikingly, at the other end of our bus route is a great new modern hospital, a kind of cathedral of healing, a wonderful monument of human skill and caring. With all its failures, humanity has come a long way from the twelfth-century leper chapel to a modern hospital.

The other day in Canterbury Cathedral I was talking to a friend about Christianity and healing. He said his views tended to be conservative about what is sometimes called 'spiritual healing', for his father had been a doctor. We agreed about two very simple things we would want to say – that Jesus was against disease, and that prayer helps. We had been talking in one of the aisles and I looked up to see some of those wonderful stained-glass windows of the thirteenth century. I noticed what vivid human experiences were portrayed there – a workman buried alive, a little boy drowning, somebody dying of an incurable disease, and St Thomas coming to the rescue as the agent of the healing, saving power of God. Where we were now standing, all those centuries ago men and women had thronged

– not as sightseers and tourists alone, but out of the pressure of deep human need. They too were concerned about 'my daughter', 'my husband', 'my son'.

Leprosy no longer takes a prominent place among the diseases of our land, but the name of Albert Schweitzer reminds us that in Africa and Asia the ancient ills live on. Recently in Strasbourg a learned conference was held to celebrate the centenary of Schweitzer's birth. There were papers read about his theology, his music, his medical skill. There was one also about his attitude to suffering. Suffering for him, it was said, was a great mystery, but he was not one of those who preach nice little sermons about the benefits of pain: to him disease was something to be annihilated.

How well that sums up the attitude of Jesus – he spent his energies royally in healing. For the common people of Galilee, like those of Cambridge and of Canterbury, came to him about 'my son', 'my daughter', 'my friend'. When he healed them their health and salvation were wonderful signs that the Kingdom of God had broken in, that in God's order these things should not, would not, exist. And Jesus sent his disciples out to do similar works, while the Acts of the Apostles show that their healing ministry continued after he was taken from them.

Throughout the centuries this healing ministry has continued, taking many forms. The spectrum range is wide, from the use of sacraments, to charismatic services and to pilgrimages such as those to Lourdes. There are those who seem to possess special gifts of healing which have nothing to do with medical training and which are effective in the no-man's-land of the psychosomatic, where mind and body inter-penetrate, and in conditions where hysteria and guilt are present. I remember hearing Sir Robert Platt, when he was

President of the Royal College of Physicians, say while a scientist was speaking about the mysterious universe: 'After all the human body is still the greatest mystery, more mysterious really than the physical stuff of the universe.'

One of the loveliest churches in Rome is dedicated to Saints Cosmo and Damian. They were Christian martyrs, laymen, medical doctors, and in the splendid mosaic we see them, clutching the ancient equivalent of their little black bags, the perennial Doctors Finlay and Cameron. They turn our minds back to Saint Luke, the beloved physician, and remind us that within the Christian Church there has been an unbroken succession of Christians who have dedicated their medical skill in an apostolic ministry of healing. There has always been an answering 'Here!' to the question, 'Is there a doctor in the church?'

'Prayer helps' – even though most of us have little idea how or why. Many large books have been written about the problem of prayer – especially about inter-cessory prayer – and we have to go on asking questions and trying to solve the problems. Yet just as illness and pain are beyond and deeper than our reason, so prayer is first of all something we just have to do. One comes back to very simple things. In the war our butcher sometimes shook his head glumly and said 'I have to look after my registered customers first.' But when we pray for those we love we have to begin by recognizing that God has no favourites for whom he keeps a special treatment 'under the counter', as we used to say. Rather, we are all his favourites so that what we ask specifically and personally by name we ask in the awareness that that is what he lovingly wills to do for all his children.

Prayer, then, is a part of faith. And anxiety, which

we cannot escape, is the opposite of faith. It is not easy to tell oneself not to be anxious, though Christian friends, Christian worship, scripture and hymns all help. Too often, to be told 'Be not anxious' is like being told 'Just relax' in a dentist's chair. But we can learn to quieten our spirits, to remind ourselves that our wants are all known to God, that we do not have to spell them out for his sake and that he loves our beloved even more than we do. And it helps to remember God's promises, to take some story from the gospels and think about it. When Martin Luther prayed his friend Philip Melanchthon back from a seizure he said afterwards, 'I rubbed God's ears with his promises!'

Catherine Winkworth, whom most of us know through her translations of the German chorales, was one of the great Victorian women. She knew a great deal at first hand of illness and pain, and in later years was able to help many friends in her letters. She once wrote:

We must learn not to look at ourselves . . . but to look at Him, to cast the care of our souls on Him . . . the more absolutely you trust him, trust your whole life and character and being, the more certain you are to find strength and guidance given as you need them. And this surrender of yourself to His will does bring peace as nothing else can: peace that takes away present conflict and discouragement for the future, because you know that now the very source of strength and of all goodness is on your side.

But praying is not something we do alone, or in a small group, or in one worshipping congregation. It is something the whole Church does all the time, in Christ. The Church is the caring community: within a vast comradeship it carries on a ministry of comfort and hope.

This is the heart of what we call *the* ministry. I remember going to what Methodists term a 'Circuit Rally' in the north of England. There was an afternoon sermon, followed by a tea. I had been met by the local minister and installed in his study before the service, and, in my academic way, had been a little appalled by the smallness of his library, just a couple of shelves. At the tea he made a long, rambling speech. During the tea the door of the little chapel opened and through it came a lady leaning on the arm of a teen-age girl. It was plain that she had been very ill and had had a good stare across that old river of Jordan. But she sat down slowly in a corner seat and then clutched her companion's arm: 'There he is! There's my minister. My friend. Every day while I was ill he came to see me. He never missed. And if I was too ill I would tap on the window and he would go away. But he was back next day.' I felt very small, for here was one who never knew how he fulfilled George Herbert's great ideal in his 'Country Parson' – 'not eloquent, or learned, but holy'. But this caring ministry belongs to all the Church, and in our prayers and in our visiting friends, it should be something to think carefully about. For there do seem to be only two kinds of visitors – those who drain us of energy and depart leaving us half dead, and those who put new life into us, do us good and cheer us up. And most of us know what it is to intend to minister, only to find that it is the one in bed who takes charge and in courage and humour gives us her blessing.

Among those papers read about Albert Schweitzer there was one about his sermons on the cross. It was, it seems, of the greatest importance for him that we put our human suffering alongside and within the sufferings of Christ. 'When the shattering experience of suffering comes, much depends,' he said, 'on how we face it . . . we should bow before it as something which can transfigure – and then suffering ennobles . . . there is a power which comes when life and death are mixed together.' R. H. Strachan in his commentary on our text says that 'the cross of Christ for Paul is a beacon for all who suffer according to the will of God. There are materials within us for an entire inversion of our attitude towards pain. A touch might transform it. One flash, one word spoken by God might suffice to make the dark places bright.'

You get the image? There are still a few ancient beacons about on high places in our land, reminding us how important they were for a nation fighting for its life. There they were, a dark, shapeless mass of bits of wood, sombre, inert, until they were suddenly, blazingly alight, shining out as a message and a sign. Pain and suffering are indeed the beacon materials of life. They can make us embittered and sour, they can poison. They can put us under such a strain that faith breaks down and hope dies. But as Strachan goes on to say: 'Paul knew that suffering of this kind is not merely purposeless, but belongs to "the pain that God is allowed to guide".' (Moffat)

That was how suffering guided another great doctor, David Livingstone. Not for him the land of counterpane, for in his last illness he trudged on across Africa much as his four soldier uncles had marched at Waterloo. Despite the fever, the bleedings, the weakness, to the very last he took his medical and scientific readings neatly and carefully. There is one lovely entry towards the end:

Caught in drenching rain which made me fain to sit exhausted as I was, under an umbrella, for an hour . . . as I sat in the rain a little tree frog, about half an inch long, leaped on to a grassy leaf and began a tune as loud as that of many birds and very sweet. It was surprising to hear so much music out of so small a musician. I drank some rain water as I felt faint.

And he added a little later: 'Nothing earthly will make me give up. I encourage myself in the Lord my God, and go forward.'

Francis of Assisi too believed that 'He prayeth best who loveth best, all things both great and small.' He has become renowned as the apostle of joy and as the author of the ecstatic canticle to Brother Sun. Yet his last years were full of pain. He was blind, and he wore a cap to hide the dreadful scars of the operation he underwent, cauterization with a white-hot iron from jaw to ears. And in his body, kept secret from his friends, were the marks of the wounds of Jesus in his hands and feet and side – so close did he come in his love to sharing Christ's sufferings for mankind. On that last journey back to Assisi they had to lift him to bless the town which he could not see, though something of that blessing has hovered over it for seven centuries. But all these things, too, were for him to the praise of the creator and he put them into that most joyful song:

Praise be to Thee O Lord for those who put up with weakness and much suffering, and blessed are those who endure such things in peace – for, O Most High, thou wilt bestow on such a crown.

COMFORTABLE WORDS

I know so well how hard the slow struggle back to life is . . . Of course it is far better than remaining ill and secluded, but it has its own sharp trials none the less. In complete illness one's life, though narrow, is intense, one's duties clear, one's heart and mind (when not too suffering) free to rise easily to God: one lives in a world of stillness, of sweet voices and tender consideration. As one comes back to the real workaday world, one slips into a more hurried, worrying, superficial life: all the jars and roughnesses come upon one, and one has forgotten how to take them lightly . . . one gets a little fussed and unreasonable . . . one begins to measure one's life by the standard of other people's . . . all the dullness and limitations of one's lot begin to tell, when the strain and acute suffering and submission is taken off and every little drawback has a sting of disappointment in it. Altogether it needs immense faith, courage and patience to get really anything like well out of a long, bad illness: but there is this comfort, one does know for ever after when one is well off, and enjoys and is thankful to the utmost for every bit of happiness and pleasure that comes in one's way.

Catherine Winkworth (1829–78)

It so happened, that one day the doctor came, bringing the iron with which he performed cauterizations for eye infections. He had a fire made to heat the iron, and when it was lit, put the iron in it. To comfort his spirit so that it should not be too greatly afraid St Francis said to the fire: 'My brother fire, noble and useful among all the other creatures which the most

High has created, be courteous to me in this hour because I loved you formerly and still love you, for the love of the Lord who created you. I beseech our creator who made you to temper your heat so that I may be able to bear it.' His prayer finished, he made the sign of the cross over the fire. As for those of us who were with him, we all fled out of love and pity, and only the doctor remained with him.

Although St Francis's illness was very grievous, he praised the Lord with great fervour of spirit and gladness within and without, and said: 'If I am going to die soon, call Brother Angelo and Brother Leo that they may sing to me of Sister Death.' Those friars came to him and with many tears sang the Canticle of Brother Sun, and the other creatures of God which the saint had composed in his illness to the praise of God and for the comfort of his soul and those of others. In this song, before the last verse, he put in the verse of Sister Death which is:

Be praised, my Lord, for our sister the death of the Body which no man living can escape.

The Writings of Leo, Rufino and Angelo

3

Our Friends Above

Hebrews 12:1. *And what of ourselves? With all these witnesses of faith around us like a cloud, we must throw off every encumbrance, and run with resolution the race for which we are entered, our eyes fixed on Jesus, on whom faith depends from start to finish.*

The New English Bible

We all grow older, we all know about pain and sickness. We are all touched at some point in life by separation and bereavement. We all have to die. Our question is, what does the Christian faith have to say about these things, and how do they relate to what we called the X-Dimension, as it is described for us in the eleventh chapter of the Epistle to the Hebrews. Let us start with the fine phrase 'the parting of friends'. The common saying 'to say good-bye is to die a little' reminds us that all our separations and partings have pain in them and point towards that final separation of death. When that comes it shocks and affronts us, for it seems to contradict what life at its most worthwhile has been about – loving and being loved. For when we love, the barriers between our lives seem to melt, and we grow into one another. We have all noticed how husbands and wives begin to talk like one another, to react to situations in the same way, often with the same words – even come to look like one another. I have seen people who look like their dogs, but that, as Kipling would say, is another story.

That we should find hurt when those whom we love die, is inescapable and natural, for it is the sign that we have really loved. If we could take such separation in our stride it would either mean that we were too thick-skinned and unimaginative to be worth knowing, or that the one who had gone was after all on the very margin of our life. The more we love, the closer we are to one another, the greater the pain. When parents die, even when they have reached great age and perhaps had a very peaceful death, there is a special grief, for our relationship with them is deep and at the very roots of our being. For happily married people, when the grim moment comes that death 'do us part', then it is the kind of separation of which Newman said: 'There are wounds of the spirit which never close – and are intended in God's mercy to bring us nearer to him, and to prevent us leaving him, by this very perpetuity.' He also said, 'There is a sorrow which grows with the years because (to use the hackneyed phrase) they become "conspicuous by their absence".' 'He just kicked the chair away,' said somebody in a shop the other day about a friend who had lost his wife, 'because he couldn't bear to see it in the place where she had always sat.'

It is a small, but real, comfort that the one who is left to soldier on alone is taking on something which otherwise his partner would have had to bear. There is no sentimentalism about this. We are talking of an experience so deep and shattering that when it comes, as has been said, 'For the rest of our journey we must creep like a wounded bird with broken wing.'

There was a time when I thought it incongruous to ask young people to sing Charles Wesley's great hymn 'Come, let us join our friends above', and especially the line 'And we are to the margin come, and we expect to die.' But I remember a youth conference in London in 1940 during a week-end when a red alert went on, a warning that invasion might be imminent. One of the younger ones gave out that hymn knowing that her brother, a medical doctor, was cut off with the army in Boulogne and that there was no news of him. In fact, more than we often realize, children and teenagers have to face the facts of bereavement and if it is the death of a beloved parent, or of friends in an accident, it is a major shock and often a challenge to faith.

What is often called 'untimely' death can indeed be something which causes bitterness or anger and can destroy faith. The first funeral I ever conducted was that of a baby, and I vividly remember sitting in the car with the sad parents behind the little coffin. It was no answer to suggest, as did in fact happen, that there would be other children to come. Perhaps one of the best answers had been given long ago in what many of you might think an unlikely place – in the British Museum Cotton MSS, *Nero.A.Ten* – which contains one of the loveliest poems of the Middle Ages. It is known as 'The Pearl' and was written about the year 1400 in the north-west Midlands. It is the story of a man whose little daughter had died at the age of two. Her name was Margaret, or Marjorie – the word meaning 'pearl'. This experience had shattered him into bitterness and angry complaining.

He tells how he flung himself down upon her grave, which was overgrown with autumn flowers, and how, in his deep grief, he was given a vision in which he saw his daughter as a lovely young woman, amid the bliss of heaven. The words may be antique, but the experience is recognizable enough:

> Deafening dolour my spirit drenched
> Though reason proffered right relief
> In fierce conflicting questioning
> My soul sank in suffering
> Though counsels of Christ all cares dispel.

The poem ends with his vision of the Heavenly City, the New Jerusalem, and with those pearly gates among which his own daughter shines as a resplendent jewel, with hope and with dedication:

> So Pearl to God I dedicated . . .
> With Christ's dear blessing and mine.

When W. R. Inge was Dean of St Paul's he became, rather unexpectedly, a very popular writer, and it was said of him that from being a pillar of the Church of England he had become two columns of the *Evening Standard*. In 1924 he wrote a Lent book which has brought comfort to many.

It was about his daughter Paula, who had died at the age of nine, having been loved by a great number of people. He wrote that bereavement is perhaps the sharpest challenge to faith in God, but that it is a challenge which faith can overcome and which can be turned to our blessing. Perhaps most poignant was the little poem with which he prefaced the book, 'Weep not for her who has been snatched away, but learn how to follow her.' He found comfort, and was able to comfort others, from what might have been a crippling experience.

Faith transforms the parting of friends into the

communion of saints. Nobody has ever put this more beautifully than the seventeenth-century Welshman poet, layman and medical man – Henry Vaughan:

> They all are gone into the world of light
> And I alone sit lingering here.
> Their very memories are fair and bright
> And my sad thoughts doth clear.
>
> I see them walking in an air of glory
> Whose light doth trample on my ways.
> My days which are at best but dull and hoary
> Mere glimmering and decays.

Love, we said, means growing together and part of that growth is stimulated by the crises of our life, of which this, separation by death, may be the greatest.

When we think about heaven some contradictory Christian notions which have arisen may occur to us. Martin Luther said: 'I shall go to sleep and I shall know nothing more until an angel knocks on my tombstone and says "Time to get up, Doctor Luther! Judgement Day!"' In a letter he wrote to his old father in his last illness he said: 'Our faith is sure, and we don't doubt that we shall shortly see one another in the presence of Christ . . . it is only a matter of an hour's sleep and then everything will be different.' I heard an old lady put the same belief the other day as she spoke to a friend: 'Well, my dear, I'm seventy-seven and you are seventy-six and one of these days, quite soon, we're going to wake up and feel all young again.'

In one of our Cambridgeshire villages there is a tiny church. It is so small that most of the space seems taken up by a family tomb, a man and his wife lying side by side and hand in hand. So lifelike are they that visitors hush as if they had walked into somebody's bedroom, and when I was there the only noise was from a little field-mouse scuttling by. There they were, a lovely image of 'asleep in Christ'.

But how, then, can we 'join our friends above' in worship? Theologians have argued much about that. It is a question too high for me, for it involves the tricky relations between time and eternity and what it really means to be 'in Christ'. To use a very crude illustration which over-simplifies: friends come to visit us and when they leave we go to the gate to wave to them as they go off down the road in their car, further and further away and then out of sight. Later they telephone to say they have got home safely – and suddenly we are in an encounter with them, here and now. Perhaps, then, we have simply to hold these two truths together – the thought of our sleeping in Christ and of the present communion of saints. The early Christians knew about this – go into the catacombs and see the little scribbles, 'Peter, pray for us! Paul, pray for us!' See the pictures of Jonah, Lazarus and the anchor, all symbols of the Christian hope. Look at the great mosaics built amid famine, flood, warfare and violence, and which are all about heaven, as though the Church in the persecutions had learned one great and unforgettable truth out of separation and death – that the visible Church is always walled around with an invisible world of heavenly glory.

Those great hymns of Charles Wesley show how this comradeship of the first Methodists bridged both sides of the great divide:

> There all the ship's company meet
> Who sailed with the Saviour beneath.
> With shouting each other they greet
> And triumph o'er trouble and death.

Multitudes of Christians would say that this is not just a pretty idea but an exhilarating experience. Nobody wrote more beautifully about this than the Puritan Richard Baxter, perhaps because he was a superb pastor and cared for men and women:

> Still we are centred all in Thee,
> Members, though distant, of one Head;
> In the same family we be,
> By the same faith and spirit led.
>
> Before thy throne we daily meet,
> As joint petitioners to thee;
> In spirit we each other greet,
> And shall again each other see.

This hope is grounded not on our perception of the meaning of life, or even our love for one another, but in the love of God for all his children, who are dearer to him than the sparrows which fall to the ground, or the grass of the field which lasts only a little day. This is a truth about which Protestants have maybe said too little, and Catholics at times too much. Yet perhaps there is a wider Christian consensus than we know. We are perhaps like two people who look up into a clear starry sky: one says, 'Ah, yes – there's the Great Bear, there is Orion; there is the Milky Way.' The other can't put names to them, but he too sees what is lovely and marvellous. The family of God is indeed one, on either side of the river of death.

Some time ago I went from West Berlin to East Berlin by underground, under the Berlin wall. It was my first visit behind the Iron Curtain by myself and I was a little fussed. I handed over my passport and papers to the men in uniform at the check-point, and then sat down as ordered, for about ten minutes. Then one of them beckoned me to the counter and said, 'We have no information about your visit. There are no papers. Nothing has come through.' I sat down glumly, wondering what to do. Then the door opened, another official came in and I was summoned again. This time they smiled and said, 'It's all right. Your friends are here. You can go to them.' And indeed, through the glass I could see my friends, the minister and his family, all smiling and waving. That is what the communion of saints is like. Our friends above cannot say of that last frontier, 'It is all right.' Only Jesus Christ can say that. But they can greet us and salute us, and we can be aware of them.

It brings us back to our text. Bishop Westcott, in his great commentary, takes up Paul's metaphor about the arena and the spectators waving the runners on. But they are more, he says, than spectators: they themselves have known the good fight of faith. And above the cloud of encompassing witnesses is Jesus, 'no Roman emperor dispensing by his arbitrary will life or death, but one who has himself sustained the struggle we bear, the pioneer and finisher of our faith.' 'Looking unto Jesus' means looking at a human being, Christ our brother, who was tempted in all points as we are, who suffered for us, and who laid down his life for his friends. The gospels show us clearly how he became a precious part of the lives of a group of men and women who were in truth his friends and his loved ones, and how he was cruelly torn from them. And though when it came to the grim test, they failed, betrayed and forsook him and ran away, he came back to them because it was inconceivable that he should do anything else. What he had begun in their lives was something which could not finally be broken because its preservation depended in the end not on them but on him. What was true of his first friends in Galilee is true of us. 'Looking unto Jesus' is what faith is about, and at the end of the day,

> We all shall commend
> The love of our friend,
> For ever beginning
> What never shall end.

COMFORTABLE WORDS

I think that those who have had to bear this sorrow will agree with me that bereavement is the deepest initiation into the mysteries of human life, an initiation more searching and profound than even happy love. Love remembered and consecrated by grief belongs, more clearly than the happy intercourse of friends, to the eternal world: it has proved itself stronger than death. Bereavement is the sharpest challenge to our trust in God: if faith can overcome this, there is no mountain it cannot remove. And faith can overcome it. It brings the eternal world nearer to us, and makes it seem more real . . . Pure affection, so remembered and so consecrated, carries us beyond the bourne of time and place altogether. It transports us into a purer air, where all that has been, is and will be, lives together in its true being, meaning and value, before the throne of God.

> W. R. Inge, *Personal Religion*
> *and the Life of Devotion* (1924)

One thing I feel deeply just now – that any true and strong affection is so much the most precious thing

God gives us, that it is impossible to believe it can be extinguished, even by death. If we can go on loving and cherishing the memory of those who are dead, it is impossible that they, who are purer and better than we, should be less constant and loving . . . when one keeps close to the great realities, one feels that they in heaven must have the same work to do that we have, to work for God and all goodness, and that the same things must be deepest for them as for us, the love of God, and the persons he has given us to love. And so I cannot help believing that it is as impossible for my own mother to forget me, as for me to forget her: and that in some way, at some time she will surely know and be happier for all the love we have treasured up for her since she went away.

Catherine Winkworth to a friend (1856)

It is a question with some, whether we shall know each other in heaven or no? Surely there shall no knowledge cease, which now we have; but only that which implieth our imperfection, and what imperfection can this imply? Nay, our knowledge shall be increased beyond belief: it shall indeed be done away, but as the light of the stars is done away by the rising of the sun . . . indeed we shall not know each other after the flesh: but by the image of Christ, and spiritual relation and former faithfulness in improving our talents, beyond doubt, we shall know and be known. Nor is it only our old acquaintances, but all the saints of all ages, whose faces in the flesh we never saw, whom we shall there both know and comfortably enjoy. Yea, and angels as well as saints, will be our blessed acquaintances. Those who now are willingly ministering spirits will willingly then be our companions in joy for the perfecting of our good: and they who had such joy in heaven for our conversion, will gladly rejoice with us in our glorification. I think, Christian, this will be a more honourable assembly than ever you have beheld: and a more happy society than you were ever in before.

Richard Baxter (1615–91),
The Saints' Everlasting Rest

4
Life

John 11:25. *Jesus said, I am the resurrection, and I am life.*

The New English Bible

I was sitting eating crumpets with an old friend when he said, 'When I got to the age of sixty I said to myself, "Now the most important thing that is going to happen to you is that you are going to die."' And he added, 'I try to live in that understanding.' Death is a fact to be reckoned with and not to be treated with morbidity or sentimentality. There is nothing of those things in the Bible, though one cannot say the same about the hymn books (Isaac Watts and Charles Wesley being the exceptions).

In some centuries death was treated with sombre seriousness. In the splendid liturgical services in the church of Saint Sophia in Constantinople, the Emperor, splendidly gowned and bejewelled, at the head of a many-coloured procession of thousands of worshippers, was presented with a little box containing dust and ashes, to remind him of the transitoriness of earthly glory. Richard Baxter in the seventeenth century kept a skull by his bedside. Throughout the Middle Ages there were tracts circulated about the 'art of dying', and in the early years of the Reformation there was a little best-seller, by Huberinus, on how to meet suffering and death. 'Fight, Christian,' it said, 'for you are not alone in this battle. Christ your king has gone along this road before you and he will protect and guard

45

you.' And the writer urged people to ponder the eighth chapter of the Epistle to the Romans.

In our time it is commonly agreed that we have had a conspiracy of silence. People avoided mentioning death and found all sorts of ways of substituting some less forthright phrase. Now, unfortunately, death is becoming an 'in' thing, to be discussed as a 'contemporary problem', and the theme of grisly programmes on television. There are magazines in America devoted to 'thanatology'. I recently read a rather off-putting book about groups of students who went round hospital wards asking terminal patients what they thought was going to happen to them when they died. There have also recently been one or two tortuous German theological studies not to be commended as cordial for drooping spirits. But there are some good books too, and one of them begins with the simple reminder that death is a subject about which nobody can speak with first-hand experience.

It is greatly to be welcomed that in our time some splendid Christian doctors and nurses are pioneers in new kinds of hospital units for the care and service of the incurably ill.

The friend who spoke of his spiritual preparation for dying was a Roman Catholic, and though Protestants might disagree with some of the forms which Catholic teaching has taken in other centuries, that teaching has always treated the subject with reverence and dignity, and made it plain that in the end Every man has to make a decision for or against God, and that this is part of an even greater decision, which is not what we think about God, but what he thinks about us. For all Christians, death, if it must be tremendous in the strict sense of a good old word, must also be something creative because of the love of God.

Jesus said, 'I am life,' and the first Christian thought about everlasting life is that it is not just something future, beyond the grave, but that here and now the quality of eternal life comes to those 'whose lives are hid with Christ in God'. 'O it is a great thing to be a Christian man,' said Luther, 'and have a hidden life, hidden not in some cell, like the hermits, or even in the human heart, which is an unsearchable abyss, but in the invisible God himself, and thus to live in the things of this world, yet feeding on him who never appears save only by means of our hearing of his Word.' The terms of reference for holy living are the same as those for holy dying.

Some of the stories about Francis of Assisi are legend but one has a ring of truth, telling of how he tackled his doctor with the question, 'When shall I die?' His doctor looked him in the eyes and said, 'I think it will be either in September or October.' Then Francis sat back with a sigh of relief and uttered his great phrase, 'Welcome, Sister Death.' But death does not come to all peacefully and gently. It may be horrifying and disgusting. The hermits of Saint Antony in the Middle Ages had a grim assignment – they had to care for the victims of bubonic plague. There was nothing they could do for most of their patients. They were doomed. A painful and disgusting death lay before them, and beyond washing their sores and carbuncles there was nothing to do but pray. But Matthias Grünewald came to their house in the Vosges mountains, and painted that terrific altarpiece which today is to be seen in the museum at Colmar.

On one side of the panel is a picture of *The Temptations*

of Saint Antony. It shows the saint beset by demons innumerable, portrayed in the mythical manner as pig demons, eagle demons, snake demons. But in the left-hand corner, shown with frightful realism is a man who has died of plague in all its physical horror. Opposite him is a piece of paper and on it the words, 'Where were you, good Jesus, that my wounds were not healed?' Here is no mythology but something very modern, or rather perennial. It is how people have always died, in inexplicable agony which is the real agony of temptation, threatening to cut the optic nerve of faith.

On the other side of that same panel, not half an inch away is the great picture of Christ on his cross. There he lies, twisted in death, with a huge crown of thorns and with his body pock-marked in a thousand places with a strange kind of 'plucked chicken' effect. His dead form hangs grey and green and hideous, against the sombre background of a black sky and a dead sea.

It is said that the hermits used to leave each new patient alone before that painting in what I suppose was a primitive form of shock treatment. Most of them would be too ill to notice, but now and then there would be one who might say, 'I am going to die, but the Son of God, my Saviour and my friend, also died in an evil and repulsive way. Yet his death became the means of good beyond any power to calculate: he will know what to do with my pain and my death.' And then perhaps he would put his soul into the hands of God and say with Christ, his brother, 'Father, into thy hands I commend my spirit.' Or as Isaac Watts puts it:

Should all the hosts of death
And powers of hell unknown
Put their most dreadful forms
Of rage and malice on,
I shall be safe, for Christ displays
Superior power and guardian grace.

Yet Christianity is not about death but about life, not about dying but about resurrection. It is about a new life, and about a God who is invincible and utterly to be trusted.

Martin Luther used to carry a little book with him in which he wrote down from time to time such comfortable words as might help him when he came to what he called 'that little hour'. But when he did come there he found he did not need the book, for he had the comfortable words by heart and they welled up unbidden in his mind.

I read the other day of a Methodist preacher who died in 1839. His name, appropriately enough, was William Smith. He was born in Wiltshire in 1758, and at the age of twenty-two was converted while a young musician in His Majesty's 28th Regiment of Foot. As a preacher he drew great crowds, and John Wesley sent him to Ireland where first in Londonderry and then in Dublin, he preached until he retired at the age of sixty-one because his health had failed. A simple obituary records:

He employed his remaining strength visiting the sick, meeting classes, and preaching generally twice a week. He read the Bible through once a year. He was able to collate the Authorized Version with the Greek text. During the last years of his life he was completely blind and his wife would read daily to him the Prayer Book liturgy, with the Psalms and Lessons and he would make the responses audibly with her. Whole chapters of the Bible and great numbers of our hymns were even at this age committed to memory and he would repeat them in the sleepless hours of the night. So in his eighty-first year, full of faith and joy in the Gospel, he finished his course with joy, saying with his latest breath, 'Glory! Glory!'

Sometimes anxiety about death is mixed up with remorse and guilt. One of the things all Christians have to do, and which they do not all understand, is to discover how to ask for and to take God's forgiveness. Our relationship with God is from beginning to end a forgiven relationship. It is not surprising, however, that some people seem to have no sense of sin, for repentance is something we learn more and more about as we grow in the Christian life, and it has been often pointed out that the saints have taught us the language of penitence. We should get into the way of making up our accounts at night with penitence and thankfulness, before we go to sleep committing our life and all those whom we love to God – and indeed, giving back to God his church and his world.

I once had the experience of going straight from the graveside of somebody most dear and close to me, to take the chair in an ecclesiastical assembly where they were discussing, with some heat, the problems of the Third World. It was like entering a bewilderingly different dimension. It was not that world problems are not important, but there is a depth in our deepest personal experiences which is the framework for all the rest. This is where the Marxists miss out. It is where the Church has a right to be heard since it speaks as a community which bestrides both life and death, and is able to interpret history in terms of that which lies beyond. When Sir Walter Raleigh was in the Tower of London as a prisoner, he got on with writing a great *History of the World*. But he had to stop for his own execution and in his last words wrote, 'O thou just, eloquent and mighty death. Thou hast taken all the far stretched out greatness of man and brought it together under those two words "Here lieth".'

You remember the story Jesus told about the man who seemed to have got on in life, who pulled down his barns only to build greater ones, and who got ready for a comfortable retirement only to be met by death when God said, 'You fool – this very night . . .!' That is not just an old oriental fable for it is happening all around us in our affluent and materialist society which assesses its quality of life in terms of its possessions. It is death which shocks us by reassessing our priorities. One of the troubadour poets in medieval France powerfully expressed the truth of the warning, 'It's later than you think.'

> What is most to be feared and for this reason I am filled with wonder, is that a man pays no heed to God until he has come so close to the evening of his days that the daylight grows dark for him, and if the daylight does not come to him then in its completeness, I do not believe he will find enlightenment afterwards.

Not long ago I went over one of the minor stately homes of England. House, lawns, parish church, winding river – these things had little changed in four centuries. Inside the house the family portraits began with Tudor paintings and ended with modern photographs which showed a recognizable family from generation to generation. Recently a film company came and made the house the centre of a modern thriller. Of course it had to be adapted, and they built around the buildings a whole new façade: a street, pubs, shops. They did it so successfully that on the screen you could not tell what was real and what was fake. Yet the difference was there and it was fundamental: part of it would endure, and part would be gone tomorrow. A member of the family would most surely have been able to tell the difference. We might well call this a parable about what the Prayer Book calls 'The deceits of the world, the flesh and the devil.' So much of our lives are spent on what in the end are trivial and ephemeral things. We are, as William Temple once said, like shop windows where somebody has switched all the price tickets round, so that what is precious is cheap and what is trumpery is costly.

The story of the raising of Lazarus has a key role in Dostoevsky's novel *Crime and Punishment*. The student, Raskolnikov, has committed the brutal murder of an old woman, and it is a turning-point in his awakening to penitence when the girl, Sonia, reads to him this story from Saint John's gospel. At the very end of the book when he has confessed his crime, and worked out his penitence in prison in Siberia, he picks up Sonia's copy of the New Testament and recalls how she had read to him the story of the raising of Lazarus. And that moment was for him, says the writer, 'the beginning of a new story, of the gradual rebirth of a man, the story of his regeneration, of his passing from one world into another, of his confrontation with a new and hitherto unknown reality, the risen Christ.' I remember vividly hearing Emlyn

Williams give an evening of readings from the works of
Dylan Thomas. For the last item a spotlight shone on a
chair heaped with the manuscripts of Thomas's poems
in the middle of an empty stage. And from off-stage
Williams read the beautiful and moving poem 'Death
Shall Have No Dominion'. Yet the moral of the chair
and the empty stage spoke louder than the words,
that death does indeed have dominion, and in the end
there is little comfort and not much explanation in the
thought that though individuals die, the race lives on.
For the rub of it is the individual. I understand why
for millions of modern men it is hard to believe in life
after death. But in the end the Christian hope is not
an analysis of life, but rather about the love of God,
that such a God as is made known to us in Jesus Christ
cannot be separated from his children.

I stood not long ago in Westminster Abbey, gathered
with Christians from many churches around the new,
black marble plaque dedicated to Gerard Manley
Hopkins. On the plaque were two words which sum
up his life, his poetry, his communicable hope: the
words 'Immortal Diamond'. Hopkins faced death with
realism for he knew the dark shadow that mortality
throws across our human life:

> Man, how fast his firedint, his mark on mind, is
> gone!

> Both are in an unfathomable, all is in an enormous
> dark
> Drowned.

But then:

In a flash, at a trumpet crash
I am all at once what Christ is, since He was what
   I am, and
This Jack, joke, poor potsherd, patch, matchwood,
   immortal diamond,

        Is immortal diamond.

There are many questions we cannot answer and about which the Bible is strikingly reticent. It has been said that too many hymns about heaven seem to have been written by tired people who seem to think of heaven as a Bournemouth from which no traveller returns. Not so Saint Augustine! When he comes to the end of his *City of God* – after millions of words about human history, he suddenly becomes tongue-tied before the splendour of heaven, and falls back on simple words:

> Yes, there in heaven we shall really retire – but only in order to see that we may love – to love that we may praise. That is what is going to happen to us in that end which has no end. For this is our final destination, to reach that Kingdom that has no end.

We have thought along with Saint John in much of this chapter. But Saint Paul must have the punch line, the ground of all our hope:

> Who shall separate us from the love of Christ?

COMFORTABLE WORDS

My Dear, first and foremost I must say that obviously the last twenty-four hours of one's life are no different from any others. I had always imagined that one would have no feeling but shock, that one would tell oneself 'This is your last sunset, now the clock will only go round twice more, now you're going to bed for the last time.' But there's no question of that . . . How good God has been to me. Even at the risk of sounding hysterical I'm so full of gratitude that there's really room for nothing else.

So then, my dear, I have only one thing to say: may God be as good to you as to me, and then even your husband's death will not matter. He can demonstrate his omnipotence at any time, when you are making pancakes for the boys, or cleaning them up. I ought to take leave of you. I can't. I ought to deplore and lament your daily toil. I can't. I can only tell you one thing. If you get a feeling of absolute security, if the Lord gives you that, which you could not have had but for these happenings and their outcome, then I am leaving you a treasure which nobody can take away.

> Count Helmuth James von Moltke in a letter
> to his wife, on 10 January 1945.

My dear, your very dear letter has just arrived. The first letter, my dear, in which you have not grasped my state of mind, my condition. No, I am not busy with the good God, or about my death. He has the inexpressible grace to come to me and to be busy with me. Is that presumptuous? Perhaps – but he will be forgiving me so much this night that finally

I dare to beg forgiveness of this last presumption also. But I hope it is not presumption, as I am not praising the earthen vessel, no, I am praising the precious treasure which is making use of this earthen vessel, this utterly unworthy dwelling place. No, my dear I am reading exactly those passages from the Bible which I should have read had there been no trial – Joshua 19–21; Job 10–12; Ezekiel 34–6; Mark 13:5 and the rest of our Second Epistle to the Corinthians. So far I have read only the Joshua and our passage from Corinthians which ends with the beautiful, familiar sentence so often heard from my youth up:

> The grace of our Lord Jesus Christ and the love of God and the fellowship of the Holy Spirit be with you all. Amen.

My dear, I feel as though I had been given absolute authority to say this to you and our little sons . . .

And now, my dear, I come to you . . . you are not just a part of the means God has used to make me what I am, rather you are me – myself. You are my thirteenth chapter of the First Epistle to the Corinthians. Without this chapter no one is really a man. Without you, my dear, I would not have had 'charity'. I do not say that I love you, for that would not be correct. Rather you are that part of me which would be missing if I were alone . . . only together do we two make one human being. We are . . . one creative thought . . . and so my dear, I am certain you will not lose me on earth, not for a moment. And we have been allowed finally to symbolize this fact of our sharing in the Holy Communion, which will have been my last.

I just wept a little, not because I was sad or melancholy, not because I wanted to turn back, but from an intensity of gratitude at this proof of God's presence. It is not given to us to see him face to face, but we must needs be overwhelmed when we suddenly realize that he has gone before us all our lives through, as a pillar of cloud by day and of fire by night, and that in a flash he suddenly lets us see it. Now there is nothing more to happen.

> Count Helmuth James von Moltke in a letter
> to his wife 11 January 1945,
> just before his execution.

Now I saw in my dream that these two men went in at the gate; and lo! as they entered, they were transfigured; and they had raiment put on that shone like gold. There were also that met them with harps and crowns, and gave them to them; the harps to praise withal, and the crowns in token of honour. Then I heard in my dream, that all the bells in the City rang again for joy, and that it was said unto them

ENTER YE INTO THE JOY OF OUR LORD

I also heard the men themselves sing with a loud voice, saying –

Blessing, and Honour and Glory and Power be unto Him that sitteth upon the throne and unto the Lamb for ever and ever.

Now, just as the gates were opened to let in the men, I looked in after them, and behold the City shone like the sun; the streets also were paved with gold; and in them walked many men with crowns on their heads, palms in their hands, and golden harps to sing praises withal.

There were also of them that had wings, and they answered one another without intermission, saying, 'Holy, holy, holy is the Lord!' And after that they shut up the gates; which when I had seen, I wished myself among them.

John Bunyan, *The Pilgrim's Progress*

Part Two

5

The Parting of Friends

A sermon to students at the end of a Summer Term

> 2 Kings 2:11–13. *And Elijah went up by a whirlwind into heaven. And Elisha saw it, and cried, 'My father, my father, the chariot of Israel, and the horsemen thereof.' And he saw him no more: and he took hold of his own clothes and rent them in two pieces. He took up also the mantle of Elijah that fell from him, and went back and stood by the bank of Jordan.*
>
> Revised Version

The Bible is full of stories about the meeting and the parting of friends, but none is more solemn than this leave-taking of the prophet Elijah and Elisha his disciple. Yet for Elisha the poignancy of departure was swallowed up in the thought of new responsibilities, a new and serious adventure. Now he had to go back alone, along the very road by which, a little before, he had travelled as a learner and a pupil. Soon he stood by the brown, swelling flood of Jordan river where on that very day he had seen a last sign and wonder, as Elijah, holding his mantle, had smitten the waters and made a safe path through the flood. And now it was Elisha's turn to stretch out his hands and with the same mantle, while in the background the sons of the prophets stared, to see what was going to happen to the new-fledged disciple, suddenly come of age.

Like some of you, I have been engaged in the last

few days saying goodbye to pupils and friends, thankful that the two circles have not been mutually exclusive. And for some of us, too, the edge of parting has been taken away by the thought of the new job.

Winston Churchill, in his book about painting, speaks of a moment when, with brush, palette and easel before you, the canvas seems to look up at you and say, 'You dare!' The Germans have a word for it: they do not ask if you have finished your studies but *Sind Sie fertig?* – 'Are you ready?'

Before all else a university is a design of persons. Every year the kaleidoscope is roughly shaken, the pattern broken, and one particular design comes to an end, never to recur. It is fitting that at such a moment Christian men and women should dedicate themselves and give thanks to God. Chesterton has said that ultimately there are two ways of looking at life: we may either take it for granted, or for gratitude. Taking things for granted is, for our generation, doing what comes naturally. Those old words, Reverence, Vocation, Responsibility and Duty belong to a past age of moral stabilities, and sound strange to a generation which has not so much lost its bearings as stopped believing that fixed points of reference exist. It is not only that so much has been done for us, not even that we have less imagination than our fathers, but that gratitude is difficult in a world where so many of our benefactors are impersonal. You cannot shake hands with a receipt in triplicate, or raise your hat to a Department of Education and Science or fall in love with the Daddy-Long-Legs of the Welfare State. No wonder if our minds grow numb, we take all we can get, behave as though we had a perfect right to it all and regard our elders with the pert, critical, half-patronizing appraisal which led James Joyce to tell W. B. Yeats, 'I'm very sorry for you: you are too old to be influenced by me!'

But here today gratitude is in order towards a God who has never been afraid of spoon-feeding his children, not grudgingly like the authorities in *Oliver Twist*, but delighting to give in double portions and then to double it again. We come to be thankful for all good gifts around us and not least that we have been made members of a great tradition.

Elijah was a great teacher, Elisha a pupil destined for greatness. The sustaining impulse that lasted down the years and enabled Auguste Sabatier to finish his life of Francis of Assisi was the moment when his teacher, the great Renan, put his hand on Sabatier's shoulder on the steps of the Sorbonne and said, 'One day you will write the greatest life of Saint Francis of Assisi.' I know that the great, inspiring teachers have always been outnumbered by the Lucky Jims, but then there has never been a majority of great, inspiring pupils. Yet betwixt and between them there has been a succession of truth throughout many centuries in which the all-important friendships between teachers and taught has been at the centre. A university where this has ceased to exist or has been made impossible, must fail in its chief end.

The great thing is the persisting of the Christian tradition of humanity and truth, a continuing partnership between generations, vulnerable and precarious, having to be renewed in each generation. So it was in the Dark Ages when two monks journeyed through the grim wilderness of pagan Northumbria to renew their vows before the deserted shrine of Saint Cuthbert of Durham, or when David Livingstone in darkest Africa made the ruins of a forgotten Jesuit chapel the place where he renewed his apostolic vocation. This great tradition is no narrow, pietistic, inhuman thing, for it has taken to itself all the virtue of the past – the glory of Greece, the grandeur of Rome, the righteousness of Israel – it will comprehend realms of truth, beauty and goodness yet unknown, since all truth was created and redeemed for us in Jesus Christ, who is the true light lighting every man coming into the world.

You remember how Archibald Grosvenor asked Patience 'Tell me, do you never yearn?' and how practical was the answer 'I y-earn my living!' A university has to strike the balance between earning and yearning, the utilitarian and the academic. We learn a great deal which is more valuable than any use we shall make of it hereafter. When, a few months hence, some of you are appalled to find how little of an Honours degree in History or English or Mathematics can be filtered through to a third form, you should remember that you were not trained to be hack job men, living from hand to mouth, but that your training was designed to make you adult men and women, holding the keys to a world of truth so that the years will mean the continual opening of magic casements rather than darkening shadows of prisons of the mind.

In the end it was the spirit of Elijah which mattered more than Elijah's mantle. During the war when two cruisers got into difficulties, the captain of one wirelessed the other 'What would Hornblower do now?' But it was not much help to Elisha to get out Elijah's mantle when he was counselling his King about the armies of Moab, or facing the Shunnamite woman with her dead son. A pile of old note books kept mainly for nostalgic reasons will count for little beside that all-important virus, the infection of truth. It is this partnership in truth which is the creative and changing thing, a symbol of the communion of saints.

For Elijah the great moment was not when with a dull flop his master's mantle fell beside him, but when he saw a vision – 'My father, my father, the chariots of Israel and the horsemen thereof' – and realized that he was compassed about with a fiery cloud of witnesses, that glorious and celestial City of God which is seated partly in the course of these declining times but chiefly in that solid estate of eternity. That is true for us, too. The great tradition of truth into which we have been incorporated is something which points beyond itself to the over-arching design of the universe, God's family, the City of God, the heart's true home.

And so we turn from the awesome Christian tradition to something simpler, the parting of friends. One of the great things about a university has been that we have made our own friends, chosen them for ourselves. And now we have to leave them, and be we never so attentive to keep our friendships in repair we shall fail to keep in touch with most of them in different jobs, across half the world and for thirty years. It is enough that for three or four years we have talked and argued. And when perhaps, twenty years on, we meet again, one a rather staid parson, and the other a respectable headmaster, it will be almost unbelievable that once we heard the chimes at midnight at the one time in our lives when high spirits do not at all depend upon alcoholic stimulus. A university is not so much a place as people, and when we return to it in after years it will be full of ghosts. When we do return, slightly patronizing and critical, of course, of those adolescent qualities we have outgrown and forgotten, we shall meet part of ourselves – and may be shattered to find, a splendid, shining irrecoverable part: our youth. This is what we now offer to God, our friendships, to the Father from whom every family on earth is named, and setting all we have done and all our hopes for the future in the context of one who went about doing good, and who laid down his life for his friends.

'To say good-bye,' says the proverb, 'is to die a little.' We are here to acknowledge the mysterious wisdom of God who is for ever disturbing, interrupting, breaking the patterns of our human loves so that every handshake, every wave of the hand, every departure, is the reminder that we are strangers and pilgrims and have here no abiding city. Yet he cheers us with the news that separation is not the final word, but rather union and unbreakable joy.

Elisha took the mantle of Elijah that fell from him and he went back. Are you ready? Thank God then that a university is not simply a preparation for life, but a precious bit of life itself. We ponder our leave-taking and our going-down as an intimation of mortality, as the reminder to each one of us that we came alone from God and must return alone to him, and that the destiny of man is to be born and live and die in the name of the Father, and of the Son, and of the Holy Ghost. And Elisha went back and stood by the bank of Jordan. As the song has it, 'One more ribber'.

> When I tread the verge of Jordan,
> Bid my anxious fears subside;
> Death of deaths and hell's destruction,
> Land me safe on Canaan's side:
> Songs of praises I will ever give to thee.

...he...
...nce done and pen...
...does come home to the little com...
...e:

> To walk together to the kirk
> And all together pray,
> While each to his great Father bends,
> Old men and babes and loving friends,
> And youths and maidens gay.

And so he learns the final lesson:

> He prayeth best who loveth best
> All things both great and small:
> For the dear God who loveth us,
> He made and loveth all.

We may not allegorize this poem in all its details, and it may be that there are in it sub-Christian elements of remorse and neurosis which do not belong to the Christian view of forgiveness. But those two chain reactions – violence, guilt, remorse and peniten... forgiveness, reconciliation – take us deep into ... meaning of the Christian Gospel for human life.

Not long after the end of the war I went i... internment camp in north-west Germany, a ... high-ranking Nazis, General Staff officers...

...re must be found a...
...ess and reconciliation – and...
opened by Jesus Christ and made possible...
I know my stumbling words were followed by...
silence.

When I come out of Bank station on the Londe...
Underground I always look towards the church of
St Mary Woolnoth and remember another Ancient
Mariner who was once its parson. John Newton ran
away to sea as a teenager and within a short time turned
into a kind of Somerset Maugham beachcomber. He
was shipwrecked and became the servant of a slave
who was the mistress of a white planter, and he tells
of his abject misery, how he crawled about in the tropic
rain, eating raw fish and roots out of the ground. Only
two things kept alive in him the memory of better
things. One was a copy of Euclid, whose propositions
he worked out in the sand with a stick. The other was
the memory of his sweetheart in England.

But for Newton too, there came a moment of break-
through, of penitence and forgiveness, and he became
...rst a sailor on a slave ship and then, with what we
...uld call a 'late vocation', took Holy orders. He
...me the great preacher and noble hymn writer
...Evangelical Revival, preaching until well over
...ears of age, because as he said, the converted
...aver could not forbear to speak of the grace

of God while he had any breath

This is the deep, evangelical about the forgiving, reconciling love of God sh to us in Jesus,
which takes away our guilt and rem and brings a
new life of penitence, a new obedient. In liberty. In
the last resort each one of us is like the Ancient Mariner,
for we are each alone in a world of our own and we
each of us have to find our way home. For each of us,
too, God has been patiently waiting, as in the days of
Noah, to bring us to our desired haven. This is not only a
message for individuals, but for the community
violence of our hate-ridden world where great com-
munities of men are shut up within a pattern of
recurring violence and suffering.

Some years ago I was in Jerusalem and made the
ascent of Mount Sion. A few hours before I read some
of the lovely verses in the Psalms about that holy
place – the joy of the whole earth, the place in which the
Lord has specially delighted. We passed through the
embattled Arab and Jewish outposts and here at last
was that holy hill. At the top stood an ancient Jew who
handed to visitors a certificate saying that on a certain
day they had made the ascent of Mount Sion. By his
side was an offertory plate, and he eyed my contribution sadly and said, 'That is a rather small offering, my
son.' But as I signed the book he cheered up, for he
saw that I came from Manchester where his daughter
and his granddaughters lived, and I assured him that,
like Mount Sion, Manchester was to me and many
others the joy of the whole earth, though perhaps it
had more than its share of the dews of Hermon. An
he waved me on into the darkness of a cave. For h
on Mount Sion was the tomb of King David – anc
never forgotten, never lost. And then in the ca
light I began to read names, thousands and th

of them under t... ords Belsen, Dachau, Buchenwald,
Auschwitz – t... ames of murdered Jewish women,
men and chi... h. There was also a poignant little
museum, a ... of soap made from human bones, a
baby's wai... at made from a page of the Talmud
taken fro... he Warsaw ghetto. And here on Mount
Sion, the ...y of the whole earth, I stood at the heart of
our age of violence.

It was crushing. But then I remembered another vision, also by a Jew. In another concentration camp, the island of Patmos, John the Divine looked up at Mount Sion and saw upon it 'a lamb'. Of all the emblems of our Lord, and indeed of our religion, surely this is a symbol most to be remembered in our time. The Lamb – the innocent one, the only human being who never added to the toll of malice and cruelty. The Lamb, the gentle one – for make no mistake, this is not a time to make fun of 'gentle Jesus, meek and mild', the one who when he was threatened, threatened not again. The Lamb who is the leader – for he has identified himself with all mankind in its solidarity of guilt and suffering, and in the blood of his cross opened out a new and better way.

One of the loveliest of medieval legends is the story of the 'Oil of Mercy'. It tells how Adam, the father of us all, was dying, and how he sent his son Seth to the gates of Paradise to beg the oil of mercy which alone could heal him. But when Seth reached the gates there was no oil of mercy for him, only an angel with a flaming sword which turned this way and that. So he went sadly back to earth, taking with him a branch om the Tree of Life which is in the midst of Paradise. found Adam was dead and he planted the blossom is father's grave. It took root and grew into a tree long, long afterwards was cut down and made into a cross, on which hung the Son of God, who is for us and all mankind, the oil of mercy.

But those who bid us look at the pain and evil, the violence and cruelty of our world, are not the only realists. Jesus of Nazareth is the supreme realist, and we may believe him when he says:

How blest are those of a gentle spirit;
They shall have the earth for their possession.

How blest are those who show mercy;
Mercy shall be shown to them.

How blest are the peacemakers;
God shall call them his sons.

The New English Bible Matthew 6.

7

The Dimension of Depth

Ephesians 3: 18–19. *With deep roots and firm foundations, may you be strong to grasp, with all God's people, what is the breadth and length and height and depth of the love of Christ, and to know it, though it is beyond knowledge. So may you attain to fulness of being, the fulness of God himself.*

The New English Bible

The train was leaving Hitler's Germany, and in the corner of our compartment sat an elderly Jew. He was very quiet until we had crossed the Dutch frontier, and then he began to speak. He had come, he said, from Austria, and now he was going to live in England – on the south coast in a place called 'Bex'll', 'Bex'll on Sea'. 'Tell me,' he said, 'is it beautiful?' And I thought of the land he had left, with its green alps and forests, and I thought of our seaside resorts with deck chairs and ice creams and a band playing *Poet and Peasant* – and then I remembered what he was escaping from and said, 'Yes, for you it will be beautiful.'

The world of the New Testament is a world of great heights and depths, of horrifying, dangerous abysses, and wonderful, breath-taking views, precipices and summits. I wonder whether Christians have not too often turned it into a kind of seaside resort, a smooth and rounded mediocrity, a life-style with no cutting edge, nothing much to distinguish us from our pagan neighbours. We know all about the dimension of width – never have Christians had wider sympathies, our minds rightly impressed with situations in Africa, India, Asia or Latin America, our consciences touched with world problems. But heaven save us from a religion which might be five hundred thousand miles wide and half an inch deep. It is about this dimension of depth that the Apostle is speaking.

'Spirituality' is an 'in' word just now, the theme of books, of conferences, and even of reports and commissions. It is concerned about the depth of our religious life. Some of the things being said about it I find rather painfully highfalutin, and I would be chary of talking to wayfaring Christians about their 'identity crisis' or 'alienation' when they have not been properly taught the meaning of the Lord's Prayer, or that most fundamental of all Christian 'know hows', how to ask for and to take the forgiveness of God. Olive Wyon once reminded us that 'God always begins with us where we are.' When Martin Luther wrote his children's catechism it was a kind of Christian ABC, and he said his prayers from it all his days. When his wife read it she said, 'Why, it's all about me!' And, she might have added, all about God, too. For our Christian life is a kind of spiral staircase, and we keep coming back again and again to the same few simple things, but at a higher level and so with a wider view. But meditation is not something utterly remote from the experience of ordinary people, who spend hours every week staring at a television screen. It has been said that planning a holiday, when the family discuss brochures, timetables, guide books, is an exercise in corporate meditation. A little while ago there was some agitation when the Tate Gallery included a small pile of bricks in its exhibition. I liked what a young art student said, though: 'I think people ought to be taught how to look and how to see.' That's a pretty good working definition of spirituality.

There was a cartoon in *Punch* not long ago, which showed a coachload of tourists high up in the Swiss Alps. They have all got out and are clustered round the guide, pressed against a fence as he points out to them, one by one, the mountain peaks. But there is one man apart from the rest. He has turned his back on them. No fence for him, and nonchalantly he dangles his foot over the mountain edge. The title of the cartoon is 'The man who had seen Everest'. He had seen the highest there was to see. Anything else must be an anti-climax. The saints are like that – they have seen God in Jesus. Like Augustine they have looked into their own hearts, into the unsearchable, bottomless abyss of the human conscience, into those dark places of our hearts where we do not go very often, and where we stay no longer than we must, but where we know that we are at odds with ourselves, with our fellows, and with God. Or like Francis of Assisi, who stared so long at the vision of Christ that his sufferings were imprinted on his own body.

But not only the great saints – recognized and remembered and recorded – tell us about the height and depth of the love of God. Herbert Butterfield in his study *Christianity and History* draws attention to the way in which in every age the Church has produced great multitudes of good men and women, who have touched the heights and depths of Christian experience and who have had profound influence on European history. Here is one of the finest stories of the Evangelical Revival:

A poor woman, that lived about ten miles from Manchester, hearing some say, 'We have been there and found the Lord,' told it to a neighbour and said,

'I wish I could go to Manchester and find the Lord!' Her neighbour said, 'Why do you not go?' She said, 'O dear child, I have no shoes.' Her neighbour said, 'I will lend you mine.' She came to Manchester on a Sunday and knew not where to go. Seeing a gentleman in the market-place she went to him and asked, 'Where is it that people go to find the Lord?' He answered, 'Come and I will show you.' He brought her to the preaching house and said, 'Go in there.' Thomas Wolfenden came to her and asked her what she wanted. She said, 'Is this the place where people find the Lord?' He went and called John Norris, one of the leaders, who took her in and placed her near the middle and advised her to look at none but the preacher. She took his advice and about the middle of the sermon cried out, 'Glory to God, I have found the Lord!', which she repeated over and over, being filled with joy unspeakable.

That is how, in the eighteenth century, on borrowed shoes and hobbling ten miles, the saints came marching in.

Such happenings could not take place, you say, in modern congregations, the charismatic movement apart. And I daresay a modern church looks staid enough, as its middle-class members put their little coloured envelopes in the wooden bowls. But make no mistake. What is going on in each heart and mind is infinitely more complex than any computer or the cockpit of the Concorde. If we could see that congregation as God sees it, it might not look so staid. It might be rather like Paddington station, Victoria or Heathrow in the rush-hour or at the height of the season – minds and thoughts rushing hither and thither, people going in different directions, most of them carrying things, from light-weight bundles, to burdens grievous to be borne, but all going places, all part of a great timetable which they did not invent, going on journeys made ready for them beforehand. So it is with the worshipping people before a God to whom all hearts are open, all desires known, and from whom no secrets are hid. He has it all under control. He knows what he is doing.

A year or so ago a student came to see me. She had been president of a Christian society in her university, had taken part in sponsored walks galore, and in demos and protests. But after three years she had come to the conclusion that philanthropy was not enough, that it could be strained and feverish if, as in her case, there was a dimension missing. She had decided to spend the next years studying the writings of the Lady Julian of Norwich. In a recent exhibition in Norwich Cathedral there was a painting of one of the most famous images of the vision of Lady Julian. She saw a hazel-nut small enough to lie in the palm of her hand: 'I thought, what may this be? And the answer came, "It is all that is made".' And in this hazel-nut she saw three properties. The first, that God made it; the second, that God loves it; the third, that God keeps it.

I remember a famous scientist talking about some theories of the origin of the universe – 'all that is made'. One theory was that the universe began as something quite small, of a size that could be held in the palm of a hand and then – woof! it began to expand and expand. And when the author of the fourth gospel speaks of the beginning of things, he too speaks of how the Word of God 'became flesh' – in a tiny baby.

I once stayed with those splendid people the Wantage Sisters. On my last morning they took me to a hut which was untidily full of drawings and bits of stone and wood, to meet a much loved Sister who in her youth had been Senior Student at the Slade. She had just finished carving figures of the Wise Men for the crypt of Saint Paul's Cathedral, the work of many years. Into the three figures she had put the Christian experience of a lifetime. The first of the Magi was standing, with his arms held before his eyes, as one seeing a great light: the God whom we meet with awe and whose majesty we behold; the God who is light and in whom is no darkness at all. The second Wise Man was kneeling, with his hands outstretched as ours might be to catch a little child who runs to us: the God who comes near to us in his manger and on his cross, the God who evokes not so much awe as wonder, at such love made homely and near. And the third – 'Ah yes, he had to be an African,' she said – lay on the ground, his arms held out in utter and complete dedication before the God whose amazing love demands our all. I cannot find a better image of what worship means, or a better illustration of our text.

In recent years student graffiti have appeared on the walls of buildings in Cambridge. Some are political, some witty, some obscure. I remember one day going to lecture and passing the Cavendish Laboratory where in the 1930s young scientists helped to split the atom. On those austere walls somebody had scribbled the words 'I love you.' Ten yards further on there was the devastating reply – 'Why?' It was springtime, and as I came back that day another way, it was through the green pastures of the Backs, with flowers of green and yellow and purple and white. It seemed to me then that the whole splendour of spring is one of God's graffiti – his declaration to us all: 'I love you' – and that what he has made, he loves, and what he loves he can keep. And all the response of his children, all the music, all the prayers, all the liturgies, all the obedience, represent that wondering response, 'Why?', about which mystery we can go no further than Charles Wesley when he wrote:

> Love moved him to die
> And on this we rely
> He hath loved, he hath loved us
> We cannot tell why.

There was a great moment in European history when, in the middle of the sixteenth century, the Emperor Charles V renounced his empire, and retired to spend his last years making his peace with God. He had ruled a mighty empire, and in the crowded church in Brussels the imperial herald read out one by one the proud titles he was giving up. But when it was all over, Titian painted the scene and he put that brilliant assembly of notables against the background of God himself, the Holy Trinity, before whom we see the Emperor casting his imperial crown. That cut him down to size, as we say. That put it all in perspective. And that, says the hymn-writer, is our goal.

> Changed from glory into glory,
> Till in heaven we take our place,
> Till we cast our crowns before Thee,
> Lost in wonder, love, and praise.

13

8

Such a River!

Psalm 46:4. *There is a river, the streams whereof shall make glad the City of God.*

Authorized Version

In the prophecy of Ezekiel there is the striking image of a stream of water which issues from the sanctuary of the Temple in Jerusalem. At first it is a tiny trickle, but it is always moving, always deepening, until it becomes a great flood; and wherever it goes, it brings new life, its waters are healing. This picture is taken into the New Testament in the vision of the City of God with which the Bible ends, and the healing stream is in the midst of it, making glad the City. Today I ask whether history so bears witness to the presence of Jesus Christ as its Lord and Redeemer? One thing is certain. If there is such a continuing, deepening, healing influence, we cannot expect it to be obvious. Christianity can never be a success story. We cannot say of it, as Mark Twain is said to have remarked when he saw the Atlantic Ocean: 'It's a success!' A religion which has a cross at its heart cannot be measured by the yardstick of human achievement, in terms of power, or moral influence, or numbers, or ability to throw its moral weight about in the corridors of power.

It is a moving experience to go down under the crypt of the Church of Saint Peter's in Rome, directly below the high altar, until one stands in a street of the third century of our era, which ran alongside the gardens of the Emperor Nero's circus. There you stand in a little street of tombs, the graves of middle-class Romans and their slaves and families, on the walls of which you may still see the emblems of their 'gods many and lords many'. Then, at the very end of the little street, there stands the tomb of the Julii with the remains of a lovely green and gold mosaic, and one of the earliest known pictures of Jesus Christ – a cross of gold behind his head, an orb in his hand, as in a chariot he ascends to God's right hand. And then you walk up a few steps, literally through the dust of centuries, until you come to a bit of red plaster and above it fragments of the great church erected by the first Christian Emperor, Constantine. Two or three steps for you, but big steps for the Christian Church in those three centuries when, as Dr T. R. Glover said, the Christians 'out-lived, out-thought and out-died' the pagan world and brought the public life of a great culture into direct relation with the Christian Church and the Christian faith.

Go up a few more steps and you face a plain altar with the words, 'Gregory I'. And now you are in a world which has collapsed, where ordered government has gone. A world of flame and flood and violence, where all must be done again and the Church has once again a world to convert – the world of the barbarian tribes, of the *gentes*.

Not very far away, in the decaying church of Saint Stefano Rotondo, you may see a marble throne with an inscription saying that in that church on a certain Sunday morning towards the end of the sixth century, Pope Gregory preached on a text from the Gospel according to Saint Matthew. That sermon still echoes down the centuries as a mark of the evangelical spirit of that great Christian, who had walked the few hundred yards from his family home on the Coelian Hill and preached the Kingdom of God in a dissolving world. He was a great organizer of famine relief and of what we should call Christian Aid (a team of Christian ladies ran a 'Meals on Wheels' service). It was a broken, elemental situation rather like Germany in 1945 as I saw it when I walked behind another noble Christian, Bishop George Bell, in the shattered frame of the Lehrter Bahnhof in Berlin, as he talked to the desperate refugees in their hunger and exhaustion. But Gregory it was who brought these British islands into the picture, when he saw the fair Saxon boys in the market-place and dispatched a mission to England, out there on the rim of the world.

So it was that in what we properly call the 'Dark Ages', and in what Sir Kenneth Clark called the 'skin of your teeth' centuries, the Church lit the light of the Gospel, and Irish and Saxon men and women built a world where beauty and learning might endure. The words 'Vandal' and 'Hun' have come down to us from those centuries and we still use them for those who, faced with beauty, say, 'Let's smash it.' But we also remember those who said, 'Because we live in a dying world, let us concentrate on those things worth keeping for ever and ever.'

But go back to Saint Peter's and walk another step or so and you come to another tomb with the words 'Calixtus II' and find yourself standing in Christendom – a world of Christian schools and universities and hospitals and St Francis of Assisi. And so walk on, up and up until you come out into the daylight before a new, white memorial tomb and on it the words 'John XXIII'. Here you can see little old ladies in black with their shopping bags praying alongside the memory of a great Christian of our time, who recalled the great institutional Church and all of us to the great and terrible simplicity of the Christian religion; that it means to love God with all our being and our fellow men with some of the love wherewith he has loved us.

Does all that sound incredibly romantic? Are we not forgetting the grim story of Christian folly and failure and indeed downright evil – the corruption of power and wealth, of the world, the flesh and the devil; the terrible war crimes of the Church militant, a record like that of Christian intolerance and anti-Semitism as evil as anything which secular history can show? Well, you know how in Benjamin Britten's *Noyes Fludde* there are two great refrains that go right through it – one the cry 'Lord have mercy' and the other 'Alleluia!'

The need for penitence is there all right. In Strasbourg there are two famous statues. The one shows Jewry, the Church of the Old Testament, a slave, bowed, manacled, blinded, leaning on a broken reed. The other the Christian Church, erect, lovely, holding her banner and her chalice. That particular image of the Church has had a battering, not least in the last two hundred years of secularization. Perhaps we should settle for one less triumphalist, and see the Church as rather like old Mother Courage in Berthold Brecht's grim play about the Thirty Years' War.

Mother Courage is the old hag who journeys in her wagon behind the marching and fighting armies, carrying out her own rather disreputable and selfish ploys in her black market. But when the tumult and the shouting dies and the captains and the kings have departed, at the very end of the day she is still there. She has survived. None can gainsay this strange persistence of the Church after dozens of moments of crisis, when its end has been gloomily or greedily prophesied by outside observers. As Sir Herbert Butterfield has said in his profound study, *Christianity and History*, if men would turn from 'politico-ecclesiastical history to the intimate life of the Church throughout the ages, and the spiritual work done by humble men over the face of the continent they would find it the most moving spectacle that history presents.' And he goes on to say that the multitude of good men and women who touch the height and depth of human experience represent a contribution to European history that far outweighs the follies and shortcomings of the Church.

In the ninth century there lived a monk named Walafrid Strabo. He was not impressive to look at, for his name means 'The Cross-Eyed One'. He had been tutor to royal princes when the political world was dissolving, and he retired to the island of Reichenau, in Lake Constance. Here, as people often do when they retire, he took up gardening, and became a kind of Percy Thrower of his age. He wrote a jingly kind of poem about his garden:

> I break the wild nettles, expose worms
> to the day
> and scatter the molehills that get in
> the way,
> And lest the good soil should drift
> out of its place
> With four bits of wood I edge the
> whole space.

A year or so ago I took my holiday nearby, and found the island of Reichenau full of vegetable and fruit gardens. And as I watched the gardeners planting lettuces with the latest mechanical aids, I suddenly saw them – those little frames, the four bits of wood to 'edge the whole space'. A thousand years later they were still doing things with the 'Strabo touch'. And then I pondered further. Perhaps I was looking at flowers and vegetables which came from seeds from seeds from seeds which were first sown by that dirty, happy little man so long ago.

Certainly that is a little parable of Church history. History still shows Christians doing things the 'Jesus way', and what they sow today in the hearts of men was sown in them from seeds which have grown from seeds which go back through the centuries to Jesus of Nazareth and Galilee and Jerusalem.

General Spears in his book *Liaison 1914* tells how he met a French soldier leaning over a bridge, staring down into the waters of a river. 'Homesick?' he asked, for he knew that this regiment came from a part of France already lost and occupied by the enemy. 'Yes,' said the *poilu*, 'and when it gets bad, I come here and look down into the waters of the river Meuse.' 'But,' said Spears, 'this isn't the Meuse, it is the river Somme! The Meuse is hundreds of miles away!' 'At home,' said the soldier obstinately, 'we call it the Meuse.' And so there is one river. Where we are in history, the little bit we know and are familiar with, our patch of time, is part of the one great stream, which makes glad the City of God.

Smetana's lovely tone poem, *Vltava* puts our image into music, for it is the story of a river, from its little gurgling beginning as a stream, growing ever deeper and wider, going through scenes of sunshine and over raging cataracts, but always moving, always nearer and nearer the great city of Prague until at last it is there, and the minor key leads into a glorious major as it flows through the city at last.

'Who knows whether such a perfect city exists?'

said Plato, long before Christ. And he added: 'The great thing is to live after the manner of that city.' But a greater than Plato, Jesus assures us that this society is no pipe-dream, that it is the goal of all human existence, that to it all things move, that it is the heart's true, final home.

The last plague of England was Asiatic cholera. It swept through England in 1832 and, among other assemblies, it ravaged the Methodist Conference at Liverpool. Some great worthies died in the following days. One of the preachers, a man hardly known, went off into the dales to preach, but fell from his horse in a little village, stricken. When the inhabitants heard that he had cholera, they would not receive him in their houses or give him shelter. His friends took him into a broken-down barn, open to the sky, and laid him on the ground in the pouring rain while one of them rode off to tell his wife and children. In his extremity someone offered him a drink, which he refused. 'Don't worry about me,' he told then, 'I shall soon drink from those streams which make glad the City of God.'

> Who can thirst, while such a river
> Ever flows his thirst to assuage?
> Grace, which like the Lord, the giver,
> Ever flows from age to age.

9

Brother Paul

Philippians 1:21. *For to me life is Christ.*

N.E.B.

On 10 August 1810 H.M. Frigate *Lively* found herself
in a desperate situation, caught in a gale off a lee
shore. The lieutenant of the watch failed to see or
hear the breakers and the ship was wrecked, though
all the crew were saved and the lieutenant survived a
court martial and eventually became an admiral. The
story reads like an action replay of the great shipwreck
at the end of the Acts of the Apostles, for it too took
place off the coast of Malta, near what is called Saint
Paul's Bay. Those of us who look back to dreary after-
noons at school or Sunday School occupied with 'the
missionary Journeys of Saint Paul', may find it hard
to believe that the truth about this one belongs with
C. S. Forester, Hammond Innes and Nicholas Mon-
sarrat.

You can get enticing brochures about the delights of
Malta as a holiday resort, but they do not usually
reprint the twenty-eighth chapter of the Book of Acts.
For those visitors met howling winds and drenching
rain, they were chilled through and through, bitten by
snakes, and succumbed one by one to the virus known
as 'Maltese Fever'.

But the people were kind, and they rallied round the
shipwrecked mariners. They huddled about a huge
fire and gossiped the news that it was a convict ship
which had come to grief. They must have noticed one

man in particular, for his back was covered with scars, and they put him down as an escaped murderer when a snake came from the fire and fastened on his arm – judgement surely catching up with him. But he shook off the snake and stood unharmed, so they thought he must be a god if you could have such a fantastic thing as a god with scars. There are stained-glass windows of the scene which show a handsome Paul decorously robed, his garments as clean as those of a film star who has been through storm and flood, but who has emerged without one golden hair disturbed. But the Paul of history must have looked a very tough character indeed, one quite at home in this grim situation (it was, after all, probably his fourth shipwreck). I begin with this picture because it shows Paul as the captain of the ship saw him and as the men of Malta saw him – as a very remarkable man.

It is hard for us, who have heard the story so often, to realize how drastic was the change when 'once, at a crash' Saul of Tarsus encountered Christ on the Damascus Road and became 'Brother Paul'. I once knew a little Jew, a Christian and lay preacher who much resembled the earliest description of Paul as a little man, with bowed legs and not much hair, and who had the smile of an angel. He had been training as a rabbi in imperial Russia at the turn of this century, and it was necessary for him to read the gospels in Greek, among other things. One night, on sentry duty in the snow outside the Winter Palace in Saint Petersburg, he read the Sermon on the Mount and in its pages met Jesus Christ. He spent the rest of his life among Jews, trying to win them to Christ. I remember going with him through some East End streets in London, and seeing him pushed and menaced by Jews who regarded him as a traitor. A great Jewish scholar has said that while Jews can write with great sympathy and appreciation of Jesus, they often find Paul difficult to take.

But henceforth for Paul life did indeed mean Christ. The little phrase 'in Christ' appears some 346 times in the handful of his writings. There was a compulsion upon him to tell others, and the story of his missionary journeys is shot through and through with his arduous travels and his manifold physical and mental sufferings.

'The style is the Man,' we say, and never was this truer than of Paul as he comes to us authentically and recognizably in his writings, which are perhaps rather like a collection of symphonies. The great commentators, Chrysostom, Augustine, Luther, Calvin, Wesley, Barth, are the Daniel Barenboim, the Maria Callas, the Peter Pears of his work – they interpret his music.

Turner said that if you want to understand his pictures you must put them all together, side by side. And when you do, they seem to fall into two main groups. There are those about the sea, about its storm and fury – you remember how he got the sailors to lash him to the mast in a great and terrible storm in order to experience what it was like from the inside, and so be able to show it to others. And then there are his skies – those wonderful dawns and sunsets, and the magic of the sunlit clouds.

There are the two great themes of Paul's letters. They are about the sufferings of Christ, which we are called to share that we may share his resurrection; and about the storm of human agony, of the doom upon men without hope because without God, and of the light breaking through. A God indeed with scars.

But they are also about the 'Christ whose glory fills

the skies' – the one who embodies the divine purpose
from the age of ages to the end of time, the one in
whom all the universe is held together. And there
are other great themes: reconciliation and love. It is
said that the translators of the New English Bible had a
battle royal one day about how to translate the word
agape in I Corinthians 13. Hundreds of years ago
translators had substituted 'love' for 'charity', on the
grounds that the word 'charity' had changed its meaning, become cheapened and inflated. But now C. H.
Dodd made a plea for its return, on the grounds that
in our time 'love' was the inflated word, grievously
caricatured in the selfish, exploiting passion of contemporary use and modern song. But love or charity –
agape is a word which has continually to be re-coined,
re-minted, and always brought back to Jesus Christ,
who shows it to us as the overflowing, self giving of
God himself.

There have always been those, inside and outside
the Church, who have thought of Paul as the man
who spoiled early Christianity by turning the simple
Gospel of the Kingdom into a terrible jungle of theological notions, from which Christianity needs to be
set free. But when we have made allowances for Paul's
own rabbinic training, for the conceptions he shared
with the thought-world of Judaism and Hellenism in
his day, there has been a great and continuing testimony
among Christians in every century that his insights
have deepened their own awareness of Christ, that with
Saint John he has been the supreme teacher. Granted,
it takes time and trouble to understand Saint Paul.
It is at least as difficult as learning Russian, but more
rewarding. And we can make too much of the com-
plexity. In the end the difficult thing about the
Christian religion is not its intricacy, but its simplicity:

not what we find hard to understand, but what confronts our souls directly with choice and action. You cannot read Paul's letters without saying to yourself: 'For Paul, life did indeed mean Christ, Christ supremely as the key and goal of all his living. What does life add up to in my account?' For it is the greatest thing about St Paul that he manages to get himself out of the picture and makes us see Jesus.

> Yea thro' life, death, thro'
>   sorrow and thro' sinning
> He shall suffice me, for he hath sufficed;
> Christ is the end, for Christ was the beginning,
> Christ the beginning, for the end is Christ.

10

Sursum Corda

A sermon at Ascension

> Colossians 3:1. *If ye then be risen with Christ, seek those things which are above, where Christ sitteth on the right hand of God.*
>
> Authorized Version

I once saw a film of a nest of birds high up on the side of a Swiss mountain. You saw the chicks, fluffy little things, fed by their mother day after day until at last there came a moment when she pushed them to the mouth of their little cave, and out – over the edge. But it was not disaster, for they flew. They were, after all, baby eagles. Something like that happened with the first Christians in the babyhood of the Church. There came the moment when their master withdrew from them, leaving them bereft and alone and inadequate. And yet the joyful meaning of the Ascension is not about the going away of Jesus, but of his continuing presence at hand.

I remember long ago seeing a mother and her little girl looking down Pall Mall at Buckingham Palace and at a line of motor cars as they entered the courtyard. Then, moments later, the Royal Standard broke out on the flagstaff. 'There, you see – ' said the mother, 'there is the flag. It means "The King has come home. He is in residence!"' Jesus Christ is not separated from us – he is with us. As the theologians say, he has taken our humanity with him. At the end of John Drinkwater's play, *Abraham Lincoln*, an actor comes to the front of the stage after Lincoln's death and says: 'Now he belongs to the ages.' That is true of all great men, but of this man Jesus it must be said, 'Now the ages belong to him.'

The picture phrase 'God's right hand' denotes the place of authority, of executive power, in the same way that we still talk about a 'right-hand man', or ask, if a friend has injured his fingers, 'Was it his right hand?' And the thought, taken from Psalm 110, is also that of some great conqueror who has won a great victory and who now takes his seat in triumph. But this is not just an affirmation of divine power and sovereignty. The Republic of Venice used to celebrate the occasion of its greatest naval victory, which was on Ascension Day. The Doge and notables of the city went out in a great ship, the *Bucentauro*, into the lagoon, and there enacted the ceremony called 'The Marriage of the Sea'. Their whole empire rested on sea power, on their dominion of the waters, and so the Doge solemnly threw into the lagoon a wedding ring – the sign that Venice and the sea belonged inseparably to one another, the reminder that the cost of victory must be eternal dedication. When we talk about the kingly rule of Christ we must remember that it is the rule of the one who took upon himself the form of a servant, who has dedicated and betrothed himself to humanity for better and for worse. The king of the Bible is the shepherd king, the good shepherd who lays down his life for the sheep.

If you read the great Collects of the Prayer Book you will notice how all the mighty acts of God in his son, which were wrought objectively in history once for all, have also their counterpart in the life of those who belong to him. As he was born, as he suffered, as he rose again, as he ascended, so we too are to be born anew, to die to sin, to rise to a new life, and to ascend to God's right hand and with him continually dwell. What God did once *for* us, now takes place *in* us.

When I was a student I once preached in a mining village near Durham, and I stayed with a family where for four generations the men had been miners, and where for four generations the men had been Sunday-school teachers. My host took me along to see their new pit-head baths, and as we went told me how in the old days they would come up out of the pit with their filthy garments and the grime thick upon them, and there in the kitchen, tired out, they would fall asleep, to awake stiff and uncomfortable.

But now he pointed to the shining sets of lockers. In the one they put their dirty clothes, and then they went into the showers, came out, and took their fresh clothes from another locker. That is how Paul sees the new life of Christians. To be at God's right hand means to 'put off' the old man and to 'put on' the new man in Jesus Christ. And in the third chapter of the letter to the Colossians he spells it all out. What we are to put on is a pattern of virtues, qualities, each with a shape, and, so to speak, a colour and a scent as any bunch of flowers, such as roses, lilacs or irises might have. They are no abstractions for they are part of the life of Jesus Christ himself, his meekness, his forgiveness, his humility, his sacrifice. But you have not understood Paul or Church history, if you suppose this to be some facile optimism, as though all the fighting were over, and there were not more wounds, more battles to be fought and won. However desperate the fight, there is above the noise of battle the sound of trumpets, the assurance of victory.

In the Tate Gallery there used to be a picture which showed Queen Elizabeth I of England and King Philip II of Spain playing chess. Yet they were not playing with chess pieces but with ships and men. When you looked at the board there was no doubt at all who would win. The little ships of England were out-manned and out-gunned by the great Armada, crowded with a formidable army. But then you looked up at the faces of the protagonists – Philip of Spain, proud, cruel and rather weak; Elizabeth of England like a female Winston Churchill, with an indomitable chin. Then you realized that this game was won before it was even begun, that it was not in the end a matter of size or numbers, but of the character of the two players. That is how the first Christians believed. They looked up to God's right hand, to Christ as conqueror and king.

During the last war, a little girl was evacuated from London during the blitz, and billeted on a famous artist. She became rather a nuisance, always interrupting his work, until one day he thought he would scare her away and so he drew on his canvas a most horrible, fearful monster. She looked at it and said, 'Coo, ain't that lovely. Now draw a robin!' It was a terrible picture, but after all it had come out of a man's head – a man she knew.

There are some frightening pictures, patterns of cruelty and violence. Yet the very worst that we hear and see around us has come out of the hearts and minds of men. And we may say of them, with Isaac Watts:

> Should all the hosts of death,
>   And powers of hell unknown,
> Put their most dreadful forms

Of rage and malice on,
I shall be safe: for Christ displays
Superior power and guardian grace.

So the ancient prayer of the early Church still rings out – *Sursum corda* – 'Lift up your hearts.' And with them we still reply, '*Habemus ad Dominum*' – 'We lift them up unto the Lord.'

11

The Abiding Spirit

Acts 2:4. *And they were all filled with the Holy Spirit.*
N.E.B.

I once visited a famous beauty spot, a Cornish fishing
village, only to be very disappointed. Something was
wrong. Then I realized that the picture postcards had
all shown it at high tide, and it looked very different
when the tide was out. The fishermen moved slowly,
heavily in the mud, putting gear into boats whose
masts stuck out at all angles, and which could be moved
only with great difficulty. Then the tide came in, and
how different it all was when tasks and problems were
caught up in another dimension. So it was with the
Church at Pentecost. The little company of men and
women, after the Ascension of their master, had been
thrown back upon themselves, suddenly conscious of an
immense task and of the pitiful inadequacy of human
resources which all the inspiration of the mighty things
they had seen had hardly changed. 'Their affection had
been tried and broken down,' said Frederick Denison
Maurice. 'It had failed towards their master: what
strength could there be in it towards any of their
fellows? If love was their own, or had its springs in
them, it must be utterly dried up. Then reflect how
it burst forth – and how they were trained to understand
that there must be about them and with them a Spirit
of very living, long-suffering love, the heights and depths
of which they could not measure, of which they could
only say "It is the Spirit of him who died upon the cross."'

In his *History of the Expansion of Christianity*, the American historian, S. K. Latourette, uses the figure of the incoming tide to describe the growth of the Christian Church. The progress of the Gospel in the world has not been a steady continuous progress, but rather a series of waves, each period of advance being followed by a period of recession. It is tempting to concentrate on those periods of advance, of flood-tide when we think of the Holy Spirit at work in history. And it is true that the study of evangelical revivals in the fifth, the twelfth and the eighteenth centuries gives ample material for meditation on the work of the Holy Spirit. Nor does it matter that these times of great renewal, of mighty works, of charismatic wonder, have a degree of what we call non-theological factors, are compassed about with the changes and chances of all history. Thomas Gray put the problem in his famous 'Elegy in a Country Churchyard'.

Perhaps in this neglected spot is laid
  Some heart once pregnant with celestial fire:
Hands that the rod of empire might have sway'd,
  Or waked to ecstasy the living lyre.

Some village Hampden that with dauntless breast
  The little tyrant of his fields withstood,
Some mute, inglorious Milton, here may rest,
  Some Cromwell guiltless of his country's blood.

So it is with Church history, with those moments when the Church militant here on earth girds up its strength and marches into battle. Such a time was the missionary outburst among the Free Churches at the opening of the nineteenth century. To get the full flavour of the story you must read those missionary dispatches as they were printed in the evangelical magazines of the period, drab, unappetizing volumes which enshrine a treasure of the Church as lovely as the Lindisfarne Gospels or the Book of Kells. Suddenly the problems of a Church world which was very circumscribed, were taken up into a new dimension. No longer is it a matter of ebb-tide or flood-tide situations for now men go down to the sea in ships and occupy their business in great waters. A narrow, middle-class sub-culture is suddenly flung on the widest of screens, top hats, umbrellas, poke bonnets, crinolines, hymn singing, Sabbatarianism, evangelical jargon and all.

But in India, Africa, the West Indies, and in the islands of the seas, great churches spring up. From Bengal to Fiji the Scriptures are translated into a score of tongues and a band of martyrs and apostolic men emerge as noble and as human as any figures in Christian history. As in a battle the gaps in the ranks are filled, the reserves thrown in almost recklessly. John Williams is murdered on the shores of Erromanga, and within months not one, but a dozen go out to take his place. Men queued up to go out and die among the fevers of the white mans' grave in Africa – as you may read on the honours board of the Methodist missionaries from Richmond College, before which Dietrich Bonhoeffer stood in silent respect. But go back thirty years and who could have conceived such possibilities? How easily, it seems, might William Carey have remained a village cobbler, John Hunt a labourer, Robert Moffat a jobbing gardener, John Thomas of Tonga a village blacksmith, and David Livingstone a factory hand. Village Hampdens all of them, suddenly involved in history, caught up into a wider pattern which they drastically and creatively changed.

But it will not do simply to look for the Holy Spirit in times of flood-tide. Talk about 'When will revival come?' or 'We need another Pentecost' is harmful if it leads men to relax the good fight of faith, or lose heart, as when little bands of Christians fight rear-guard actions in areas left by a moving population, or when a whole bundle of sociological conditions lead them to feel on the losing side, and to question their own faith. Or when any one pattern of renewal is taken as the sole method by which the Holy Spirit must work in the future.

Professor Coulson once reminded us of how often and banefully in the history of science, God has been introduced at the point of some gap in human knowledge. And in Church history the Holy Spirit has sometimes been called in to fill the blanks. But the deepest significance of Pentecost is not to be found only in great moments of renewal or in sudden divine interventions, but rather in the abiding presence of the Holy Spirit in turning the ordinary stuff of our common humanity into the Holy Catholic Church.

When we consider the first Christians and their humble origin, there is about the divine economy an apparent casualness which is in the strict sense of the word, awful. Napoleon chose his marshals from those who were proven veterans of many battles. A modern expedition to the Poles, Mount Everest or the moon, gathers its members with great care, sifting out thousands of technical qualifications. But for the salvation of mankind, Jesus of Nazareth strolls a few miles from his own village and chooses his team from a group of peasants and fishermen, some apparently his own relatives. Had he not called them, they would have remained in their trivial anonymity – a village Peter, two or three mute, inglorious evangelists, a Judas guiltless of his master's blood. The Jewish and Roman authorities had no doubt about it, these followers of a small-town prophet were simply small-time stuff. In the weeks which followed the death of Jesus they made no attempt to round them up. Yet on the day of Pentecost these little people took over history: they began from that date to supersede Jewry, to challenge the Roman Empire. They were involved in a new solidarity, the fellowship of the Holy Spirit.

When we see God dealing this way with the men and women of Cana and Capernaum, we feel they might have been born in Gray's Stoke Poges, Stanley Spenser's Cookham or Rupert Brooke's Grantchester. But then we remember that this is precisely what God has been doing ever since – that it is out of such human material that he has built his Church. There is truly something shattering about its simplicity, the smallness of the human pattern. It is there in the teaching of Jesus in his emphasis on being faithful in small things, and in the promise that one day the little things – like a cup of cold water – will be seen in their true, eternal significance.

There is a clue here as to why men and women have again and again found inspiration in turning to the New Testament picture of the primitive Church. It has meant many things in Christian history, from the Desert Fathers to the Franciscans, the Anabaptists to John Wesley or the Oxford Movement. All in one sense rediscovered a primitive Church which never was. And yet they saw something, true enough to provide a cutting edge with which to criticize and to begin a practical programme of renewal.

This abiding presence of the Holy Spirit in the Church calls for and gets no headlines: it is unromantic and unexciting. For in the Church of Jesus Christ it is always washing day and the Holy Spirit in the midst is always at work with his grimy, weary business of washing away men's sins, of comforting broken hearts, and wiping tears from his children's eyes.

The great Puritan, Richard Baxter, in his *Life of Faith* gives some twenty marks of the continuing work of the Holy Spirit and he ends:

Suspect not all church history or tradition, in extreme opposition to the Papists. Our tradition is . . . nothing but a certain history or usage of the universal Christian Church, and therefore it is to be lamented exceedingly that these . . . are not sufficient without the testimony of the Holy Spirit, as if all this were none of the testimony of the spirit.

To stress the continuing work of the Holy Spirit in ebb as well as in flood-tide situations is theologically important, for it underlines the faithfulness of God and the unchangeable trustworthiness of the divine promises. Not only in the fervour of the revival, or of a charismatic congregation, or amid great flourishing churches can men find the encouragement of the Holy Spirit. The small band of men and women in some desolate downtown church in the inner city, the damp running down faded walls, trying to cope with ebb-tide situations amid machinery invented in time of flood – they too may rejoice:

Our glorified Head
His Spirit has shed,
With his people to stay,
And never again will he take him away.

Our heavenly Guide
With us shall abide.

But, as the great Schoolmen and Karl Barth remind us, not less important than the divine faithfulness is God's sovereign freedom. The Spirit moves, as they say, *ubi et quando* – where and as it pleases him. We properly speak of the gift of the Spirit remembering that it is the essence of a gift that it is free and unconstrained and might never have been given at all. So the Holy Spirit abides in the Church in constant faithfulness and freedom.

That was a great moment in English history when a ragged army of desperate common men marched on London in 1381, and when suddenly the young king rode over to the side of the rebels and said, 'I will be your leader!' The Holy Spirit is God coming over to our ranks, to our side, as our true Leader; always a move ahead, always preparing us for coming tasks, always assuring us in every desperate hour of final victory, giving us new light on our problems, right judgement in our decisions, and the most holy comfort of his abiding presence.

> Then let us rejoice
> In heart and in voice,
> Our Leader pursue,
> And shout as we travel the wilderness through.

12

Treasure Trove

A Sermon preached at the Leys School, Cambridge

> Proverbs 2:3. *If thou criest after knowledge, and liftest up thy voice for understanding: if thou seekest her as silver, and searchest for her as for hid treasure: then thou shalt understand the fear of the Lord and find the knowledge of God.*
>
> *Revised Version*

We have most of us read *Treasure Island*, but I wonder how many of us could say what they did with the treasure when they found it? I looked it up, and found that Robert Louis Stevenson disposed of that in a couple of lines: 'All of us had an ample share of the treasure, and used it wisely or foolishly according to our natures.' That is, Jim Hawkins, Dr Livesey and Long John Silver went on being themselves, and the kind of people they were determined how they spent what they had discovered.

The Bible speaks of wisdom as a kind of treasure. When it so speaks it is not of something remote or theoretical, but of a kind of practical 'know how' – the understanding which enables a man to live as God means him to live. Education, too, is a kind of treasure hunt, and all that well-meaning stuff about schooldays being the happiest days of one's life has got that much truth in it. A good many of us forty years on, looking at our contemporaries and ourselves, would have to say with Stevenson, 'We all had our share . . . but we used it foolishly or wisely according to our natures.' This applies above all to the great tradition of truth, beauty, and goodness which we have received from the past – a tradition always precarious and vulnerable rather like the Wells Fargo gold coach in some Western film, which is always liable to be hi-jacked and so lost. But this tradition has rather marvellously carried on through many centuries, taking into itself the glory that was Greece, the grandeur that was Rome, and the righteousness and compassion which we owe to Israel and the Christian centuries.

This is indeed a great treasure, and in it each member of the Christian schools of this country has a share, for it is a partnership in excellence. It is for each of us to decide, whether, for our part, we hand it on, enriched by our possession of it, or cheapened and impoverished. One of the grisliest places in England is the chapel of Saint Peter in Chains within the Tower of London. For it is where centuries ago the great traitors who had been executed, were buried. Not the little men who sold their country for money, but men and women of royal blood, of nobility, of eminence in Church and State, who stood so near the heart of our national life that they could inflict on it a deadly wound.

Here their bodies were flung into the ground with shame and humiliation. For they had laid hands on treasure and thrown it away. And this very word 'traitor' reminds us how in the days of the early Church there were *traditores* who in the time of the persecutions handed over to the Roman soldiers the precious copies of the Holy Scriptures which it was their office to guard for the Church – the Church which they thus betrayed. So the words 'tradition' and 'traitor' are close to one another. We can hand on or we can throw away.

A few years ago I was going into Westminster Abbey when I saw a schoolboy being ignominiously led out by a verger. He had been scribbling his name and the date on the wall outside the Chapel of Henry VII – shall we say 'Johnny Green – day, month, year'. Well, that was one way of dealing with him, taking him gently by the ear and putting him out of the door. Another way might have been to take him round the chapel, to show him the tombs of Queen Mary and Queen Elizabeth and the little children of James I; and then out among the graves or memorials – Winston Churchill, David Livingstone, the musicians, the explorers, the statesmen, the poets – and then to take him up into the triforium to look down from where the great carpets look like postage stamps. Then he might be taken down once again to look at his cheap little bit of vandalism – 'Johnny Green'! And yet there was a sense in which he was right, after all. For each one of us can in fact put our name and date to all that is great and noble in our history. It does all belong to us, and we to it. It is a treasure in which we all share. There was a cartoon in *Punch* some time ago which showed them bringing the school milk. But the milk float had broken down, and so between it and the school there was a long line of schoolboys each chucking the bottles from one to the other. But at the very end of the line there was a terrible mess of broken glass and spilled milk – you see, the last boy couldn't catch and so it didn't really help that every one of the others had taken hold and passed on – for it all stopped at this point. And so to us, at the end of the great chain, there comes responsibility.

Our text speaks about seeking for wisdom, about a persistent, growing search. There is one thing about which there are no examinations, but which is at the very heart of education. It is that restless bug in the mind, which is called curiosity.

There have been long periods of history when intellectual curiosity was regarded as a part of original sin, but surely it is an indispensable virtue. Curiosity, they say, killed the cat. Well, as Shakespeare says, she should have died hereafter. But curiosity discovered penicillin and built the sputnik. Curiosity crossed the Atlantic with Columbus, sailed round the world with Drake and Anson, crossed Africa with David Livingstone, went to the Pole with Amundsen and Scott, scaled Everest, and landed on the moon. And this is something which needs to persist and grow, so that as the years go on there are always new windows opening in our minds, and not, as there are for many people, only the slamming, one by one, of magic casements. Not long ago we had an application in the University of Cambridge from a lady of over eighty wanting to enrol for a research degree. We did not laugh, nor were we patronizing, but humbled and abashed at this reminder of what the search for wisdom is about – that in the deepest sense we have to be at school all our days.

But come back to ourselves – to now. One of the silliest things said to the young is that 'real life' only begins when we get out of school into the 'real world'. How often, losing an argument, do the words come from our elders, 'When you are as old as I am, my boy . . . !' Or 'One day, you'll realize that what I am saying is true!' It's a very difficult thing to reply to, apart from going hot under the collar and walking out, or with the deadly retort, 'If you were only as young as I am –

but that you can never be again!' But in a very important sense, what happens in school is 'real life'. Those years between fifteen and twenty-five will bring experiences of joy and sorrow more sharp, more acutely tasted, more full of happiness and pain than in the after years. In these years when we are learning to think straight (which is hard), and to feel straight (which is much harder), and to take account of God and of our fellow men (which is hardest of all), very important things are happening to us. That is why Wordsworth, when he was seventeen, used to like to go and stand by some great waterfall, because its rushing, tormenting, beautiful power answered the boiling and teeming of thoughts and feelings in his own mind.

> He was o'erpower'd by nature,
> By the turbulence subdued of his own mind
> By mystery and hope,
> And the first virgin passion of a soul
> Communing with the glorious universe.

Here, now, you are to learn the great lessons: to love truth and justice, not for yourself but for all men; to hate all shams and hypocrisies; to loathe cruelty, oppression and mindless violence; to speak and act decently and honestly; to listen without cynicism or cowardice to the call to serve others and sacrifice for the common good. Here, now, you encounter God in Jesus Christ and know what it is to be ashamed and forgiven, and to be commissioned to go out in his name and in the power of his Spirit.

There was a great headmaster of this school, and when he died they found a bit of paper in his pocket on which he had written some words of the poet

Whittier, which say better than anything I could say about the great succession of truth and of our part in it:

> Others shall sing the song,
> Others shall right the wrong
> Finish what I begin
> And what I fail of, win.
>
> Hail to the coming singers,
> Hail to the brave light bringers
> Forward I reach and share
> All that they sing and dare.

Acknowledgement

The author is grateful for permission to quote from the following work:

Balfour, Michael & Frisby, Julian: HELMUTH VON MOLTKE (Macmillan, 1972).